The Story
of Canada

The Story of Canada–a **Childcraft** title
(Reg. U.S. Pat. and T.M. Off.–Marca Registrada)

© 1995 World Book, Inc. All rights reserved. This volume
may not be reproduced in whole or in part in any form
without prior written permission from the publisher.

World Book, Inc.
525 W. Monroe
Chicago, IL 60661

Printed in the USA

ISBN 0-7166-6456-9
LC: 95-60195

1 2 3 4 5 6 7 8 9 10 99 98 97 96 95

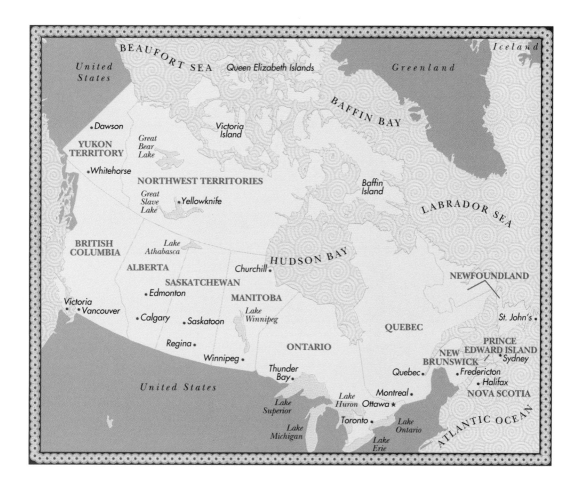

The Story of Canada

World Book, Inc.
a Scott Fetzer company
Chicago London Sydney Toronto

Consultants:

Professor David Jay Bercuson
Department of History
University of Calgary

Professor John Dickinson
Department of History
University of Montreal

Assistant Professor Roger Hall
Department of History
University of Western Ontario

World Book wishes to thank the following individuals
for their contributions to **The Story of Canada**:
Gerry Bailey, Donna Cook, Kelly Shea Doherty,
Irene Keller, and Heather Mills.

Contents

The first Canadians

The hunters looked at each other and grinned. Then they glanced again at the sprawling plains ahead. They had never seen anything like it. The plains were alive with animals and birds. There were musk ox, elk, mammoth, and many more. Never before had the hunters seen herds like these. The months of trekking south through ice and snow had been well worth the effort.

The first people to live in Canada arrived about 15,000 years ago. They walked from

what is now Siberia. At that time Alaska and Siberia were joined by the Bering land bridge—a piece of land across the Bering Strait. They made their way south through an opening, or corridor, in the ice sheet that stretched across the top of the continent. These prehistoric people were nomadic, or wandering, hunters. They hunted caribou, elk, mammoth, and other large animals.

By about 10,500 years ago, they had settled all over North and South America, south of the ice sheet. As the ice age ended and the ice sheet gradually retreated northward, the hunters went with it.

Hunters of the north

The young Indian pointed to a small path in front of him. It was certainly a deer track, and it looked as if deer still used it. This would be a good place to build an enclosure, where they could trap wild herds.

Soon the Indians were busy putting up a strong fence made of brush. Then, inside the enclosure, they built smaller fences so that it looked just like a maze. Finally, here and there they placed a snare made of tough strips of deerskin. When it was finished the Indians were pleased. They would catch many animals here.

These Indian hunters of the north lived in the vast lands that stretched from the MacKenzie River to the Labrador coast. They lived in small groups and constantly moved from one hunting ground to another. Most of the tribes spoke either Athapaskan or Algonquian.

The hunters used what they found around them to make clothing, weapons, and objects such as ceremonial masks. They used wood from the trees, bones and skin from animals, and stones from the ground. Weapons were very important tools. The hunters used bows and stone-tipped arrows, stone-tipped spears called lances, traps, and snares.

The men of the tribes made the weapons for hunting, and the women made the snares and traps. Women also made bone needles and bone and wood scrapers. The scrapers were used to prepare animal hides and furry pelts for use as clothing. Containers were made from wood and bark, and some rough pottery was shaped. Homes called lodges were made of animal skins, bark, or brush placed over a cone-shaped frame of poles. Up to 14 people could live in a single lodge.

Bark from birch trees was used to make canoes. These lightweight boats were easy to repair and to carry, and they floated high in the water. They were especially useful along rivers where there were rapids and waterfalls. Northern Indian canoes could hold two adults and a cargo weighing 116 to 140 kilograms.

The Feast of the Dead

Carefully the men dug the grave. They dug it deep enough to hold all the bodies, as well as the animal skins and household items offered to the dead. Then they built a raised platform along the grave's edge. Now all was ready for the Feast of the Dead.

The Feast of the Dead was very important to the Huron, an Iroquoian-speaking people who lived south of Georgian Bay. People from many villages joined in. Such ceremonies and rituals allowed them to make new friends and to feel part of the Huron nation. The Huron nation was made up of five tribes, each of which looked after a part of Huron territory.

The Huron believed that most things in the world had a spirit. One was the sky spirit, who ruled the weather and helped those in need. But lesser spirits could also help human beings as well. All Huron asked the spirits for help in hunting, harvesting, and war.

When the ceremony began, the bones of the dead were carried to the platform. Then the grave was lined with beaver skins and robes. On top of this they placed a layer of pots, pipes, beads, wampum, and other things, which were given by relatives and friends of the dead. The bones were then tipped into the grave, more beaver skins were placed over them, and the grave was covered with tree bark, earth, and wood. The ceremony made sure the dead would have the spirits of these objects with them in the next world.

After the ceremony, the feast began. The Huron provided food from their own farmlands as they lived mainly off the produce they grew. This included corn, beans, squash, and sunflowers. They also ate fish and meat, which was often whitefish and venison.

People of the buffalo

The scrawny jack rabbit pricked up its ears. It could hear a dull rumbling sound in the distance. The rumbling grew slowly louder. A great herd of buffalo was moving across the plain like a huge brown wave. The jack rabbit scampered away.

The buffalo might have been a danger to the rabbit, but it meant everything to the Plains Indians. It provided food, shelter, and things with which to trade. The buffalo's skin or hide was made into clothing. Skins were also used to cover tipi lodges.

The sinews, or tendons, of the buffalo were used to make bowstrings for the hunters, and

Tipi lodges were often made of buffalo skins over poles.

the animal's stomach made a wonderful kettle. In winter the kettle was filled with snow and held over a fire. As the snow melted, more was added until the kettle was full. Then it was tied with string or plugged.

The women of the Plains tribes were good at dressing and painting hides. But the women of a tribe called the Mondor, who lived to the south, were even more skilled. So the Plains Indians traded unpainted hides, robes, and dried meat with them for painted hides, feather ornaments, headware, and dried corn.

At first, buffalo were hunted on foot. But after the Spanish brought horses to North America, the Plains Indians used them to make the hunt quicker and more efficient.

Fishermen and traders

Low waves rolled gently across the sea. Tiny specks of sunlight danced across the grey-blue water. Then, with a crash like thunder, a big whale broke through the surface.

Nearby, a dugout canoe bobbed and dipped as the wave made by the whale passed under it. The hunters inside began to row with all their might. When they had pulled as close to the whale as possible, the harpooners struck. The kill was made and the huge mammal lay still. Now it would be towed to shore and its great bulk used for food and oil.

The Indians of the west coast were great fishermen. Some hunted whales. Others caught porpoise, otter, and seal. However, the most important catch of all was salmon.

Salmon were caught in various ways. Nets and lines worked best, but hooks and smaller dip nets were also used. Salmon were plentiful, and many were preserved for the long winter months by smoking or drying.

The west coast Indians were also great traders. And they built wonderful dugout canoes, some of which were 20 metres long with room for 60 men.

Each tribe was divided into villages. The Indians built their houses from cedar planks, and several families occupied each house. Outside the houses stood tall totem poles.

The people of each village were divided into three groups—nobles, commoners, and slaves. The chiefs came from the group of nobles. When a new chief was appointed, a special ceremony called a potlatch was held. At the potlatch, the new chief gave away valuable items to show how wealthy he was.

The story of Messou

Unlike other men, Messou did not hunt with dogs. Instead, he hunted with powerful lynxes, which he called his 'brothers'. One day Messou was warned that a nearby lake would turn out to be dangerous for his animals. Not long after, while Messou was hunting an elk, the lynxes chased the elk into the lake. When Messou arrived at the water's edge, he looked for his brothers everywhere but could not find them. Later a bird told him that it had seen the lynxes at the bottom of the lake held prisoner by monsters!

At once Messou leaped into the lake. But as he did so the lake began to overflow, and soon its waters covered the whole Earth. Messou was shocked. Now his entire world was gone. He stopped searching for his lynxes and began to think of ways to create a new world.

First he sent a raven to find a piece of earth. The raven dived in, but the earth was so deep in water that he could find nothing. Then a muskrat came. He swam down and at last was able to bring back some earth. Messou thanked him, and from the earth he made a new world.

Later Messou changed himself into a thousand different animals to punish the monsters that had taken his lynxes. Then he married a little muskrat, and their children brought the new world to life.

With stories like these, the native peoples tried to explain the mysteries of the universe. The story of Messou is somewhat like the Bible story of Noah and the Flood.

The first Europeans

The Viking storyteller raised his hand to silence his listeners. Then he began to tell his tale. It was a story his audience liked very much—the story of Leif Ericson and his voyage to Vinland.

The story, or saga, tells how Leif set sail from Greenland in about the year 1000 and made his way west. Eventually he came to the east coast of Canada. He called the place he had found Vinland, and spent a winter there.

There are many Viking stories about voyages to North America that took place after the Vikings had settled in Greenland. They were great seamen and loved the adventure of discovery and trade.

We know for certain that Greenlanders came to Newfoundland because a Viking settlement has been excavated in that province at L'Anse aux Meadows. This Viking site and the Viking stories together suggest that these adventurers may have explored much of the east coast of North America, including Baffin Island and Labrador.

They may also have come into contact with the native Indians. The Indians probably defended their territory against the Vikings, who often looked very warlike. It is likely, though, that the Indians also traded with the Vikings.

The Vikings stopped coming to Canada later in the 1000s. They left their homes in Greenland around that time, probably because the climate became very much colder.

L'Anse aux Meadows is on the northeast tip of Newfoundland. It was the first Viking settlement found in North America.

The merchant venturers

In the 1500s, the English city of Bristol was a great trading centre. Local products were traded for imported goods such as wine, fruit, sugar, and spices. So not surprisingly, the most important citizens of the town were its merchants.

The merchants lived in tall stone-built houses four or five storeys high. They lived very comfortably on their profits. But they were always looking for ways to make more, especially by trading with eastern countries for spices and luxury items.

At that time, though, the journey to the east was long and difficult. The merchants had learned that you could get to the Spice Islands of the east by sailing to the west. They also knew that a large land area stood in the way. That land was North America.

Some believed there must be a quick way round or through this land. So they sent ships to look for a passage to the east. Of course, the passage was never discovered. But other things were found, including fish and beaver skins. The fish were caught off the Grand Banks of Newfoundland, and the beaver pelts were traded from the Indians.

Other merchants, from France, Spain, and the Netherlands, began to send ships regularly to North America. Sometimes the merchants grouped together to raise money for their ventures. Although they did not find an easy passage to the east, many merchants from Bristol and elsewhere became richer through the new trade with the New World.

Newfoundland fishery

The sailors were pleased with their day's work. Early that morning they had gone to sea in their small boats to fish for cod. Now they had brought their catch back to shore. Later it would be shipped to Europe.

After the voyages of John Cabot in 1497 and other explorers in the 1500s, fishing in Newfoundland waters became very important to European countries. Annually, hundreds of ships came to the Grand Banks, as the fishing grounds were now called.

Some sailors used the dry fishery method, where fish were laid out on racks to dry. Their bases for cleaning and drying the fish were set up on shore.

Others used the green fishery method. They cleaned and salted fish on board ship.

The salted cod did not fetch as much money as the cod processed in the dry fishery, but green fishery sailors could make two trips to the Grand Banks each year, instead of the dry fishery sailor's one.

Most sailors from England and northwest France used the dry fishery method. Sailors from southwest France often used the green fishery method.

24

Cartier's men put up a
cross on the Gaspé Coast.

River of Canada

Jacques Cartier's men worked hard. They made a cross 9 metres high and on the cross-bar they placed a shield with three fleurs-de-lis on it—symbols of France. Above the shield they fixed a board on which was written, 'Long Live the King of France'. When the cross was put up, Cartier and his men knelt down in front of it and worshipped God.

The cross was put up in 1534, at the entrance to a natural harbour on the Gaspé coast. Some people think that Cartier claimed the land for France by raising the cross. Others do not agree. They believe the cross was used simply to mark the position of a good natural harbour. Cartier had already put up other crosses for this very reason. Also, he had not been sent to claim the land for France and did not have the authority of the French king to do so.

Cartier's job was to find a passage to the east and to discover land where gold might be found. He was given money by French merchants for his voyage.

Cartier made voyages in 1534, 1535-36, and 1541. Each time, he sailed down the St. Lawrence River, getting as far as where Montreal is today. On all his journeys he met and traded with the native people.

Cartier did not find a passage to the east, nor did he discover gold, but he did learn a lot about the geography of the land. And he provided it with a name—Canada. 'Canada' was an Iroquois word that probably meant 'village'.

Father of New France

Samuel de Champlain was pleased. The buildings he had ordered built looked solid enough, and the fortifications would give adequate protection. Champlain's aim was to start a settlement in the interior of Canada that would survive. And this 'Habitation', as the settlement was called, built near the foot of Cap Diamant, was just the beginning.

Samuel de Champlain arrived in Canada in 1603. That year, he sailed up the St. Lawrence to Montreal with the French explorer François Grave du Pont. Then he became part of the Port Royal Colony on an inlet of the Bay of Fundy. Although this colony was abandoned, Champlain felt sure that an inland colony could survive. He reasoned that it would be much closer to the important fur trade. Champlain was finally given permission to start a new colony on the St. Lawrence and thus the Habitation was built.

Most of Champlain's men died of scurvy that first winter. But the survivors became the start of Canada's first permanent European settlement. New France was about to grow, and the city of Quebec, which grew up around the Habitation, would be its centre for many years.

Champlain worked hard to make the colony strong. He promoted the fur trade, made successful alliances with the Huron, and fought against their enemies. He became a great explorer and geographer. He died in Quebec in 1635.

The Long Sault

The cries of the Iroquois warriors rang out. But now there was no reply from the Huron or French. Most of them lay dead!

The Huron had fought well, but some braves had gone over to the enemy. The French had stood firm until the end at Long Sault, west of Montreal, but neither the French nor the Huron could stand up to the Iroquois. The battle was over.

Long before, the Huron and the Iroquois had become enemies. The arrival of the Europeans made things even worse. Both the Huron and the Iroquois traded for furs with the northern tribes, but the Huron supplied theirs to the French, and the Iroquois to the Dutch and English.

Both Indian groups became dependent upon European materials, and this lead to a great rivalry for control of the fur trade. The result of this rivalry was the Iroquois wars, fought between the 1640s and 1660s.

The Iroquois soon saw the Huron as a threat to their control of the fur trade and set out to destroy them. In just over 10 years of bloody wars, they achieved that goal.

Farming became dangerous because of Iroquois attacks, and the fur trade almost came to a standstill. But New France survived, as the Iroquois were weakened by their own losses.

The Society of Jesus

Some missionaries died at the hands of the Iroquois when Huron land was attacked.

The Jesuit missionary stood among the silent Indians and looked grimly at the child nestled in his arms. He knew the infant had smallpox and would soon die. Nevertheless, the Jesuit slowly raised his hand and baptised the child. There was nothing else he could do to help.

The Jesuits were a group of Catholic priests whose full name was The Society of Jesus. In the early 1600s they believed they had important work to do in North America, helping and praying for the settlers and teaching the Native Americans about God and his son, Jesus Christ. They worked among the Huron and other tribes and built missions like St. Marie on the shores of Georgian Bay.

Life was very hard for the Jesuits in Canada. Travel was difficult and they had to eat food seasoned with salt or spices that they were not used to. They were certainly far from the comforts of life in Europe. Also, they had to try to understand the ways of the Indians, which were very different from their own. But the Jesuits were determined, and ready to die for their beliefs.

At first the Huron did not trust the Jesuits. They did not want to change their way of life or their religion. And they knew that the Jesuits, like other Europeans, brought fatal diseases such as smallpox and measles.

Some Jesuit missionaries lost their lives while working in North America. But the Jesuits did not give up. They continued to do their missionary work and to encourage other Europeans to settle in Canada.

A royal colony

The settler beckoned to his wife, then looked again at the man approaching on horseback. "Could it be Jean Talon?" he thought. But what could the Intendant want with him?

The settler's wife came to the doorway. She assured her husband that all was well. The

Intendant needed to take the census in New France. This occurred in 1666, three years after the King of France officially took over the colony. New France was brought under royal control to help stop the Iroquois from attacking the settlers, and to provide France with raw materials such as fish and furs. The French army had been sent to fight the Iroquois, and many soldiers had been persuaded to stay on as settlers.

Other settlers arrived too, but there were few women among them. So the King of France ordered that women should be found who would be willing to live in the colony. The women were expected to marry when they got there. Many did, and, as children were born, the colony began to grow.

Two officials made sure that the colony was run properly. The governor supervised the armed forces and acted as the king's representative when dealing with native peoples and other nations. The Intendant looked after the colony's courts, money, and business affairs. As the colony grew, the Intendant had to carry out more tasks—such as the taking of the census.

The seigneurial system

The sails of the windmill turned slowly in the breeze. Below the open doorway of the mill stood a habitant farmer along with his horse and cart full of sacks of wheat. Soon the wheat would be carried into the mill and ground into flour. The mill belonged to the 'seigneur', who was the owner of the land. The habitant farmer was the seigneur's tenant, so he used the seigneur's mill.

In New France people were given land through a method called the 'seigneurial system'. It had begun in Europe in medieval times when great lords ruled the lands and peasants worked for them. In New France, the company that controlled the colony for the king hoped that giving land to important

The important men, called seigneurs, were given land which was called a 'seigneury'. Each habitant farmer was then given a strip of land, which when passed down as an inheritance was divided into thinner strips.

men would persuade these men to pay to bring out settlers, or habitants, to work it. But few seigneurs did this, so the settlement spread out gradually from the main cities, Montreal and Quebec.

The seigneur, who was often a wealthy merchant, military officer—or even a religious institution—had to rent land to anyone who wanted it. The seigneur also had to provide a mill where wheat could be ground into flour. The habitant's most important duties were to pay rent and to pay certain taxes.

The seigneurial system was not a great success in helping the settlement grow. Often the landlord did not want to spend money bringing settlers over to New France. But eventually the long, narrow farms did become the heart of French-Canadian country life.

Marie de l'Incarnation

The small Indian girl looked up at the smiling lady in front of her. The lady seemed strange, dressed in clothing that hid everything except her face and hands. But the girl knew the lady was kind and good. She always smiled and helped the children learn.

The kind lady was a nun called Marie de l'Incarnation. She had been born in France in 1599 and was well educated and good at practical things. But more important to the Catholics were the visions she had seen. One night she had dreamt that God had come to her and said, "Do you want to be mine?" She answered, "Yes". From that moment, Marie wanted to become a nun.

Marie did not take her vows immediately. In fact, she first married and had a son. After her husband died, she gave her son into the care of her sister-in-law and brother-in-law and became an Ursuline nun.

After working in France, Marie felt that God wanted her to go to Canada. So, in 1639, she sailed to Quebec with a rich Frenchwoman called Madame de la Peltrie and two other nuns. Madame de la Peltrie gave money to help Marie build a convent and boarding school in the city of Quebec. The building was constructed in 1642, but unfortunately, it burned down on the last day of that year. However, more money was raised and the convent and school were rebuilt.

Marie ran the convent and taught the Indian children and the children of the habitant farmers. She also learned Indian languages very well, which helped her to communicate with the native peoples.

Marie wrote many letters—it was the only way of communicating over distances at these times. Her letters tell of her life and the way people lived in Canada. When she died, most of her letters were sent back to her son, who became a monk in France. Many can still be read today.

Acadia

The first people to settle successfully in Acadia, now New Brunswick, Nova Scotia, and Prince Edward Island, were French. They came in 1604 and lived close to the trading posts on the Bay of Fundy. Later they were joined by Scots and Irish people.

The settlers had to cope with the strong tides of the Bay. These tides rise and fall over 15 metres, so the settlers made dykes, or barricades. The dykes kept the waters out and created areas of rich and fertile land. In time, the settlers built better dykes and were able to grow wheat and raise livestock.

Although the Acadians were French in origin—as were their governors, army garrisons, and priests—they did not use the French seigneurial system of farming. They traded with the British colonists of New England rather than the French colonists of Quebec. And after 1710, when Acadia came under British rule, the Acadians stayed neutral.

The Acadians accepted British rule, but decided that they would not fight against the French. This neutral way of life seemed to work well, until the Seven Years' War between France and Britain that finally ended French government in Canada.

The coureurs de bois

The men had paddled hard and long through waters both rough and smooth. They had carried their canoes and equipment across slippery rocks and through forest tracks. Now, at last, they had reached their destination. But the journey was only half done. Soon they would have to paddle back to Montreal. The men could not face the return voyage. So, secretly, they sold their souls to an evil spirit. And it, in return, lifted their canoe into the air and flew the weary men home!

This is the story of La Chasse-Galerie, one of the many stories told by the canoe-paddling traders to help pass the time.

After the Iroquois were defeated, the French in Canada took over the job of trading with the northern Indians for furs. The men who first did this job were called 'coureurs de bois', meaning 'runners of the woods'. They exchanged everyday goods such as metalware and textiles for furs, then brought back the furs to Montreal.

Making a living was not easy for them. They had to paddle for hours and carry their canoes overland between stretches of water.

The coureurs de bois worked mostly for themselves. But by the 1700s their place had been taken by the voyageurs—men hired by merchants to deliver goods and pick up furs. They were not independent, but their task was just as hard as that of the coureurs. They sang songs and told stories like La Chasse-Galerie to make their journeys seem shorter.

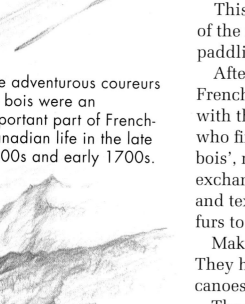

The adventurous coureurs de bois were an important part of French-Canadian life in the late 1600s and early 1700s.

Westward!

The water of the huge bay seemed to stretch northward forever. Médard Chouart, Sieur des Groseilliers and Pierre Esprit Radisson were delighted. Here, they thought, was a route that would lead into Hudson's Bay and on to Europe. It would make a much better trading route than the old Montreal—St. Lawrence route.

Explorers like Radisson and Groseilliers saw the chance to build a fur empire trading with Europe. But when the king of France did not approve of their ventures, they went to England. There they persuaded King Charles II to sign an agreement called a royal charter. The charter allowed a group called the Company of Adventurers Trading into Hudson's Bay to set up in business. The group later became known as the Hudson's Bay Company. Trading posts were soon established on the bay.

Other explorers were led by trade and commerce to push west. Rene-Robert Cavelier, Sieur de la Salle, explored the upper Great Lakes. Then he travelled down the Mississippi to the Gulf of Mexico.

Much later Pierre Gaultier de Varennes, Sieur de La Vérendrye and his sons explored as far west as the Rockies. They helped open up a huge new fur territory.

In the 1700s the push west slowed. Nevertheless, the explorers had begun to open up the country and show just how vast and interesting Canada was.

The gentleman governor

Louis de Buade, Comte de Frontenac, stood in the Chateau Saint-Louis with a group of French officers. Facing him was a British officer, Major Savage. Savage looked squarely at Frontenac and asked him to surrender Quebec to the British. Frontenac thundered, "I have no reply other than from the mouths of my cannon and muskets!" It was a grand reply and the British, on that occasion, did not take Quebec.

Frontenac was governor of New France from 1672 until 1682 and again from 1689 until 1698. He was a proud and elegant gentleman who liked to live well. He was also a bold commander.

Unfortunately, his grand life style led him into debt and he needed to make money from the fur trade to help out. He was very interested in the trade generally and helped to encourage its growth. In 1673 he founded Fort Frontenac, where Kingston is today. The fort was supposed to hold an army garrison but was in fact a successful trading post. Frontenac used some of his profits from trade to help adventurers like Cavelier de la Salle in their trading expeditions.

Frontenac's thirst for expanding the fur trade led to difficulties with the Iroquois. When the British went to war with France in 1689, their Iroquois allies attacked settlements around Montreal. Then in 1690, a British fleet sailed up the St. Lawrence to Quebec. But Frontenac's men fought off the British and saved the colony.

Frontenac was often criticised for his temper and for his life style. But under his rule the colony prospered.

The forges at Saint-Maurice

The population of New France had to grow if the colony was to survive. Jean Talon, the first Intendant, knew that. He also knew that the colony could not grow without new industries such as ship-building and iron-forging. But there were not enough people in New France to support the new ventures Talon tried to start, and the products made were too expensive to sell in France. So these industries failed.

Intendant Gilles Hocquart was more successful. He encouraged important merchants from France to come to Canada, and they brought enough money with them to get new industries started. In 1739 an iron foundry called the Forges de Saint-Maurice was built near Trois-Rivières.

In Quebec, a naval shipyard was established. It received money from the French government to help it build warships for France. But private ship-builders could use the yard as well.

Most industry in New France was carried out by small family firms. The artisans, or skilled craftsmen, often worked alone or with just the help of an apprentice. An apprentice spent three to seven years working for his artisan boss. Then he might start up a business of his own.

Artisans such as carters, blacksmiths, and barrel-makers were important in the growth of New France.

The Acadians

The British officer looked at the Acadian family as they walked slowly toward the waiting ship. The family had been forced to leave their farm. Now they must leave their country as well.

The officer said a few words to some soldiers nearby, who then took hold of the mother and father and marched them forward. The panic-stricken children were led in another direction. The smallest child broke down and sobbed. But the soldiers continued. They knew that the parents would never see their children again, as the children were each bound for a separate destination.

Many families were separated in this way when the Acadians were forced to leave their homes. The problem had started when Britain and France went to war. The Acadians were French settlers living in an area controlled by Britain. Most were peaceful farmers who, after Britain had taken over, wanted to be neutral and not fight on either side. Also, they refused to take the British oath of allegiance. Then some Acadians were forced to fight for the French. The British then ordered all Acadians rounded up and sent to British colonies along the east coast of America.

Thousands of Acadians were sent away. Many reached the British colonies to the south, but some died on the way, mostly of disease. Some stayed in the colonies they were sent to, while others made their way to the French Caribbean or to Louisiana. A number were sent back to France.

After the war, a few Acadians came home, but it was not the same. Their farms had been taken over by 'New England' settlers. So the Acadians settled in new areas of Nova Scotia and New Brunswick.

Nova Scotia and Newfoundland

The merchant ran his finger down a line of figures in a large book. When he reached the last figure, he smiled. Trade had been good and his profits were higher than expected.

The merchant lived in the new town of Halifax in Nova Scotia. The town had been founded in 1749 when 2,500 settlers and two regiments of soldiers had arrived from Britain. The first settlers had faced many hardships, but the town had survived and grown. It was helped when New Englanders from Britain's colonies to the south settled along the Nova Scotia coast on lands that had belonged to the deported Acadians.

Halifax soon became Britain's most important naval base on the Atlantic coast. This helped the town's merchants, who were able to sell goods to the British navy and army. Some of them became very wealthy.

Newfoundland began as a British colony in 1583, but its population grew slowly. For the most part, Newfoundland was used as a British fishing base, with St. John's as its most important settlement.

The British might not have tried to set up a colony on Newfoundland at all if it had not been for the continual wars with the French. But the island gave the British a base. Some French settlers tried to start their own colony on the south coast of the island, but it did not survive. However, the British allowed the French to fish in Newfoundland waters and dry their catch on the north and west coasts.

The siege of Quebec

The British soldiers stood in one long line on the Plains of Abraham. They faced east toward the city of Quebec. As the French soldiers came into range, the skilled British soldiers aimed their muskets and fired.

Musket balls cracked through the air in both directions, but the British soldiers had the best of it. French rule in Canada was about to end.

In 1754 Britain and France were fighting in North America even though they were not officially at war. At first the French were successful. But the British fought back, and in 1758 captured Louisbourg, the important French fort on Cape Breton Island. Now they wanted Quebec.

The city was defended by the Marquis de Montcalm, a French soldier who did not believe Canada could be saved. But then, Montcalm did not know how to use the Canadian militia and Indian allies to prevent the British army from advancing.

The British army was led by General James Wolfe. Wolfe tried a daring move, taking his troops up the steep slopes that lead from the St. Lawrence to the Plains of Abraham. It was a terrible risk, as there was no way of retreat.

When Wolfe's redcoats were arranged in their single line, Montcalm rushed his troops forward rather than waiting for reinforcements. The fighting did not last long. Wolfe was killed and Montcalm died of wounds. Quebec fell and a year later Montreal surrendered. New France was soon to become the British province of Quebec.

Revolution!

Throughout the winter, the American soldiers huddled under the walls that protected the city of Quebec. They had tried unsuccessfully to take the weak British garrison that stood inside. Then the weary Americans learned of a British fleet sailing up the St. Lawrence. The American general, Benedict Arnold, realised that he had no chance of winning Quebec, so he marched his soldiers back to New England. The siege of Quebec had failed!

The people of the Thirteen Colonies had grown increasingly discontented since the British conquered New France. The British wanted to tax their colonists more to pay for their costly wars, which the colonists felt was unfair.

In 1763, Britain and France signed a peace treaty called the Treaty of Paris. It said that France must give up all her land in North America except the small islands of St. Pierre and Miquelon. But even though New France became the British colony of Quebec, most of the people who lived there were still French.

The British were well trained and highly disciplined.

Britain knew that this could be a problem. So the Quebec Act, passed by Britain in 1774, guaranteed French Civil Laws, the freedom to worship in a Roman Catholic Church, and that Roman Catholics could hold office. It also allowed for rule by a governor and council without an elected assembly. The Quebec Act did not please the people of the Thirteen Colonies. They felt that all British subjects had the right to an elected assembly. They also objected to the fact that the Quebec border was moved further south, stopping the colonies from growing.

In 1775, colonists and British soldiers came to blows in a battle at Lexington and Concord. This was the beginning of the American Revolution.

The Americans were ready to defend their homes and families.

The colonists hoped that the people of Quebec and Nova Scotia would join them in their struggle against Britain. But most Québécois were suspicious of the Americans. Quebec and Nova Scotia stayed loyal to Britain and so became the foundation of what is now modern Canada.

The Loyalists

The tall-masted ship drew closer to the Nova Scotia shore. On board, the passengers were quiet. They looked tired after their difficult journey, but they were happy to be so near the land they would soon call home.

The passengers were 'Loyalists', and they came from the Thirteen Colonies during the American Revolution. They were called Loyalists because they had refused to fight in the Revolutionary Army. Instead, they had remained either neutral or faithful to King George III of England. At all times on their journey they risked being captured and sent to prison by American soldiers, so they had to be wary.

When the Loyalists reached what was now called British North America, they were given land by the king. A man and his wife received a lot, or piece of land, of 809 hectares. A single man got 20 hectares, and to make things fair, lot numbers were written on pieces of paper called certificates and usually put into a hat. Each settler pulled out one certificate. The certificate he got told him which piece of land was his. No one knew, of course, how good their land was going to be. As well as land, the settlers received free provisions until they could provide for themselves.

Most of the Loyalists were farmers and artisans. Few were very rich, and many had to struggle to survive. But survive they did and today, many Canadians are descended from the original Loyalists.

Montreal

Lake Huron

Kingston

St. Lawrence River

Toronto

Lake Ontario

Mohawk River

Hudson River

Lake Erie

New York City

Many Loyalists came to Nova Scotia, but others went north along the Hudson and Mohawk rivers to settle along the St. Lawrence River and in Quebec. Still others settled in the Niagara region of what is now Ontario.

Upper and Lower

Ahead, the forest looked dense. But the men had cut their way through worse land, and they were determined to build the road. The men, known as the York Rangers, worked under Governor John Graves Simcoe. He knew that Upper Canada needed careful development if it was to succeed, and this meant giving it a capital city, a proper land survey, and roads.

The Loyalists who went west settled in the Niagara Peninsula and along the Upper St. Lawrence River. They were used to British government and did not want to live under French civil law or to be part of the seigneurial system. So in 1791, the British government divided old Quebec into two colonies—Upper Canada and Lower Canada. The dividing line was the Ottawa River.

John Graves Simcoe was sworn in as Upper Canada's first lieutenant governor in 1797.

Upper Canada, west of the Ottawa, was ruled by a lieutenant governor and a council. There was also an assembly elected by the people, but it had little power.

East of the Ottawa, Lower Canada had a governor who chose his council from among the most prominent English-speaking colonists.

The seigneuries were allowed to continue, but all other land was to be owned by the Crown. It was divided into townships and sold to settlers, although the best lands were given to local companies based in Britain. These companies were supposed to encourage emigration, but some waited for the price of land to rise, then sold it to Canadian settlers.

The general store

"And finally", said the customer, "I'll have a half-pint of lamp oil". The storekeeper nodded and brought him the best oil he had. Then he added it to the pile of things the man had ordered. There was pepper, sugar, tea, soap, starch, fish hooks, two pairs of stockings, and a new horse collar.

When the customer had discussed his bill, he went to sit near the big stove in the middle of the store. He told the storekeeper how his farm was getting on, and in return the storekeeper told the man as much news about the village as he could.

A general store in the early days of the Canadas was more than just a shop. It was a centre where people could meet and talk. As trade between Britain and its colonies increased, more goods came into the general stores, and the stores became more popular.

In Upper and Lower Canada, as well as in Nova Scotia and New Brunswick, farmers became more prosperous. They sold more of the things they grew, which in turn allowed them to buy more goods.

A general store stocked everything from knives and spoons to hats, mill saws, and toys. It usually gave credit to local families, and sold produce from nearby farms. And it provided luxury items for the few people who could afford them. So everyone in the community liked to go to the general store.

To the Pacific

Alexander Mackenzie looked at the vast
ocean in front of him. Then, on a nearby rock,
he wrote these words: 'Alexander Mackenzie
from Canada, by land, the twenty-second of
July, one thousand seven hundred and ninety
three'.

Alexander Mackenzie had finally done
what many explorers and traders before him
had failed to do. He had reached the Pacific
Ocean by an overland route from the Canadas.

In the mid-1700s, the fur trade was growing and traders were moving westward. Some thought it would be easier to ship furs from these western regions from bases on the

Pacific. But no one had yet found a way through to the great ocean.

In 1792, Alexander Mackenzie set off to find such a route. He journeyed from Fort Chipewyan in what is now Alberta to the Slave River, the Great Slave Lake, and then by an unknown river to the sea. But the ocean he found was the Arctic, not the Pacific. Mackenzie was bitterly disappointed. He called that unknown river the 'River of Disappointment'.

But the tough Scot did not give up. In 1793, he set off again. This time he had better equipment, and after crossing the Rockies through the Peace River Pass, he finally reached his goal. An overland route to the Pacific had been found.

The Nor'Westers

A light mist hung over the glassy lake as the canoe came around the point. It was much longer than the Indians' three-man canoes, being 12 metres long and 2 metres across the middle. Inside the first canoe, a team of men paddled like a well-oiled machine. The Ojibwa on the shore watched in silence as one canoe followed another. The only sound was the splash of the paddles and the smooth swish of the boats as they glided swiftly through the water.

Canoes like these were called 'canots du maitre'. They were used by the fur traders of

the North West Company to transport goods on the Great Lakes. The North West Company started up in 1779, when groups of Montreal fur traders joined together to form one large association. The traders wanted to do this to make the transport of goods between the western fur lands and Montreal much cheaper. Cost was all-important, as the North West Company had to compete against the Hudson's Bay Company.

The North West Company supplied the voyageurs who paddled these canoes with provisions like pemmican, corn, wild rice, and fish, so the difficult journey to the west was made bearable. The North West Company went on to do well in the fur trade.

Competition with the Hudson's Bay Company was so fierce that it nearly ruined both firms. However, by 1821, the Hudson's Bay Company proved to be the stronger, and it swallowed up the North West Company. The two companies joined together under the name of Hudson's Bay Company.

As well as the 'canots du maitre', the North West Company also developed the smaller 'canots du nord'.

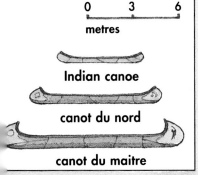

0   3   6

metres

Indian canoe

canot du nord

canot du maitre

The War of 1812

On October 13, 1812, nearly 1,300 American soldiers prepared to cross the Niagara River and invade Upper Canada. They boarded 13 boats, made the crossing, and marched toward high ground nearby called Queenston Heights.

Waiting for the Americans was an army of British soldiers, Canadian militia, and Indian allies. They were led by a brilliant fighter— General Sir Isaac Brock. As the Americans moved forward, Brock and his men charged. Brock was killed almost immediately, but this so angered his troops that they fought harder than ever. Eventually the Americans were driven back. Their invasion of Upper Canada had failed!

The Battle of Queenston Heights was just one of the battles fought when the United States declared war on Britain in 1812. The United States invaded the Canadas not only because they were British colonies, but because a great number of people had moved there from America. The Americans thought

Indian allies played an important role in defending Canada. Chief Tecumseh of the Shawnee led several thousand warriors in the Detroit region and south of Lake Erie. In 1812, he helped prevent an invasion from the west by intercepting supply convoys. He died at the Battle of Moraviantown in 1813.

these people would not support Britain, making the colony easy to conquer. But they were wrong.

The war was part of a greater struggle between Britain and France. The United States joined in because they wanted more land, because they thought Britain was supporting Indian border raiders, and because some Americans supported France. But mostly they joined because the British navy was stopping and searching American ships on their way to Europe. It seemed like a second War of Independence.

However, the war, which lasted until 1814, did not accomplish much. The Americans believed they had won, the Canadians thought they had won, and the British did not consider it important anyway.

Timber

The raft men, or 'drivers', leaned heavily on their long oars. The steering oar bit into the water and kept the huge raft moving forward. The raft, made of long lengths of squared timber lashed together, drifted slowly past the mission church on the Oka reserve. The men, who had lived on the raft ever since it set out from Hull, were pleased as the worst part of the trip was over. Now Montreal and Quebec lay ahead.

Rafts like these were built to move timber from forests along the Ottawa River to timber stocks in Quebec. In the early 1800s, the timber trade had become one of the most important industries in the Canadas. It began when Britain started taxing timber that came from countries outside the British Empire. This made it very profitable to ship timber from Canada to Britain. Also, in Lower Canada, the seigneurial lands had become overpopulated, and the settlers began to move into the Ottawa and Sagueney valleys. Many farmed in summer and worked in the forests in winter.

There were many new jobs in the timber trade. Lumberjacks cut down the trees and squared the logs. Teamsters hauled the logs to nearby rivers, and drivers floated the logs down local streams to the Ottawa. There the logs were bound together into rafts and rowed downriver to Quebec. The timber was stacked along the shore, then loaded onto square-rigged ships. Hundreds of these ships came to Quebec each year.

The immigrants

A small child lay against the stained and foul-smelling wooden wall of the ship's hold. Around him crouched members of his family, and others who had been there on the four-week voyage. The people were packed into such a small area they could hardly move.

The boy looked very sick. His mother sat nearby but said nothing. She knew that the boy had cholera and probably would not live to see Canada. Many people had already died on this awful journey.

Most immigrants to Canada in the first half of the 1800s were from England, Scotland, and Ireland. Most were poor, and so were bundled into the filthy steerage holds of ships used to carry timber from Canada to Europe. These ships were overcrowded and unsanitary, and cholera was a constant fear. When the immigrants landed they were put into quarantine at Grosse Ile, near Quebec, where they died like flies.

Many of the immigrants were unemployed people from Britain. In 1831 in Montreal, almost 50 percent of the workers were of British background. This meant that Lower Canada now had a community made up of many different cultures, not just French.

The number of immigrants made the population grow quickly. Between 1817 and 1851, the population of Nova Scotia grew from 81,000 to almost 277,000. Upper Canada's population increased from about 100,000 to over 950,000.

The pioneer farmers

Susanna Moodie looked out across the fields of tree stumps. In the distance she could see her husband, John, swinging his axe. The blade dug into another broad tree trunk. Susan looked at the tree stumps and at the grass that grew between them. "When will the land ever be cleared?" she thought. "When will the work ever be done?" She sighed and went back to the endless chores of a pioneer wife.

Susanna was one of many well-bred people who emigrated to the Canadas. Some had enough money to buy cleared land to farm. But the Moodies had to clear their land themselves and put up with all the hardships pioneers had to face.

The Moodies first moved to a farm near Cobourg, east of Toronto township. But John was a soldier and knew little about farming, so they did not do well. In 1834, they moved to Duoro township, north of Peterborough. Both of them found pioneer life difficult. But eventually, they cleared their land, planted crops, and made a success of their farm. Luckily, though, John was made sheriff of Hastings County in 1839 and so the couple moved to the small town of Belleville. This suited them much better.

In Belleville, Susanna Moodie began to write about her life as a pioneer woman. Her best-known book is called 'Roughing It in the Bush' and tells about the difficulties of pioneer life. Later she wrote 'Life in the Clearings'.

The circuit rider

The crowd grew silent. They had been waiting for almost an hour. Now he was here. Some of the younger people had never heard the preacher before, but they had often heard about him. He was a big man with a powerful voice, and everyone thought he was the best Methodist preacher in the Canadas.

The preacher walked slowly forward. He took his place on top of the little hill at the far end of the field. Then he raised his right hand and began to speak. No one took their eyes off him until he had finished!

A preacher was one of the most important people in pioneer Canada. He might be Presbyterian, Baptist, Methodist, or Roman Catholic. He might preach in a log church or in the open air. But when he came along, he was the centre of attention.

Methodist preachers, known as circuit riders, travelled from community to community. When they had preached to every community on their circuit, they started all over again. The Methodist preachers, who sometimes came from the United States, helped build a strong Methodist Church among the pioneers.

Sometimes the preacher spoke at a great outdoor get-together called a 'camp meeting'. The camp meeting often took place on a public holiday, making it even more exciting.

The Church of England was more solemn. Its ministers tended to preach in towns. The formal ways of the Church of England made it less popular in pioneer communities.

The waterways

The man took off his shirt and threw it aside.
This was hot work. He lifted his shovel and
began to dig again. Sweat dripped from his
forehead as the shovel plunged into the earth.

This man was one of many who worked to
build the Welland canal system. This system
would allow boats to travel between Lake Erie
and Lake Ontario. Until then, the mighty
Niagara Falls had made that trip impossible.

In the early 1800s in British North America, travel by road was very difficult. The roads were poor to start with and they became worse during the spring thaws. So the best way to travel was by water. Rivers and lakes were natural waterways, but sometimes it was necessary for men to make their own.

The most important waterway in the Canadas was the St. Lawrence-Great Lakes system. But there were white-water rapids on the St. Lawrence near Montreal, and shallows between Montreal and Quebec, not to mention the great Niagara Falls. In 1825 a canal was built around the Lachine rapids or the St. Lawrence. Then in 1829, the first of four Welland canals was dug to take boats around the Falls.

As water transport became more important, large open boats called 'bateaux' replaced canoes between Montreal and Lake Ontario. After 1810, steam-powered boats made travel easier on rivers and canals.

By 1848, a string of canals bypassed the St. Lawrence rapids, and the Welland system had been made larger. Also, the Rideau Canal had been dug to connect Lake Ontario with the Ottawa River. This helped the transport of goods—not only within the colony, but between the Canadas and the west.

Steam across the Atlantic

It was 2 o'clock in the morning of July 17, 1840. From Halifax docks, the watchers saw the lights and the dark, shadowy shape of the approaching steamship. It was the Britannia, 12 days out of Liverpool and carrying the royal mail. The Britannia was the first scheduled steamship to arrive in Halifax.

By the mid-1800s, steamships had improved a great deal. In 1833, the first steamship crossed the Atlantic. It was the Royal William, using auxiliary steam. This meant the ship had a steam engine as well as sails, and was therefore not totally dependent upon the wind or the weather.

A businessman called Samuel Cunard built up a great steamship line. He believed that steamships were better than sailing ships because they could cross the Atlantic on a fairly precise schedule. This would make carrying cargo much more efficient.

In 1839, Cunard asked the British government if he could start a mail service from Liverpool to Halifax, then on to Boston. The British government agreed and gave him £55,000 a year for 10 years to get the project underway. In 1840 the Britannia made its famous voyage. Mail and passengers were unloaded at Halifax and on the ship went to Boston.

Industry

John Redpath watched as the men unloaded huge barrels of sugar from the steamship. The sugar had come from the West Indies and would be refined in Redpath's new refinery in Montreal. The refinery, built beside the Lachine Canal, was an impressive building with a huge smokestack and outbuildings.

John Redpath was born in Scotland in 1796. He came to live in Montreal, where he worked as a stonemason, building small houses and stores. Soon his business grew. He signed contracts with the British army, the government, and the Roman Catholic Church.

John Redpath and his men helped build canals, warehouses, churches, and military posts.

This earned Redpath a lot of money, which he used to start other industrial projects. People who use their money, or capital, in this way are called capitalists.

Montreal began to develop as a centre for industry, which meant that raw materials were made into goods there. Shoemaking, for instance, became an important industry. So shoes were made in the town, rather than imported from England. This changed the way people worked. Instead of one man producing goods to order, several worked in a shop, making products in standard sizes.

New inventions and technological discoveries helped this growth in production. And immigrants worked for very low wages. This kept the cost of production low and allowed the capitalists to make more money.

By the 1850s, capitalism and industry had helped make Montreal Canada's biggest city.

Family Compact

John Strachan walked through the door of his elegant Toronto house. It was a fine building and it certainly reflected his position as leader of the Church of England in Canada and member of the Family Compact.

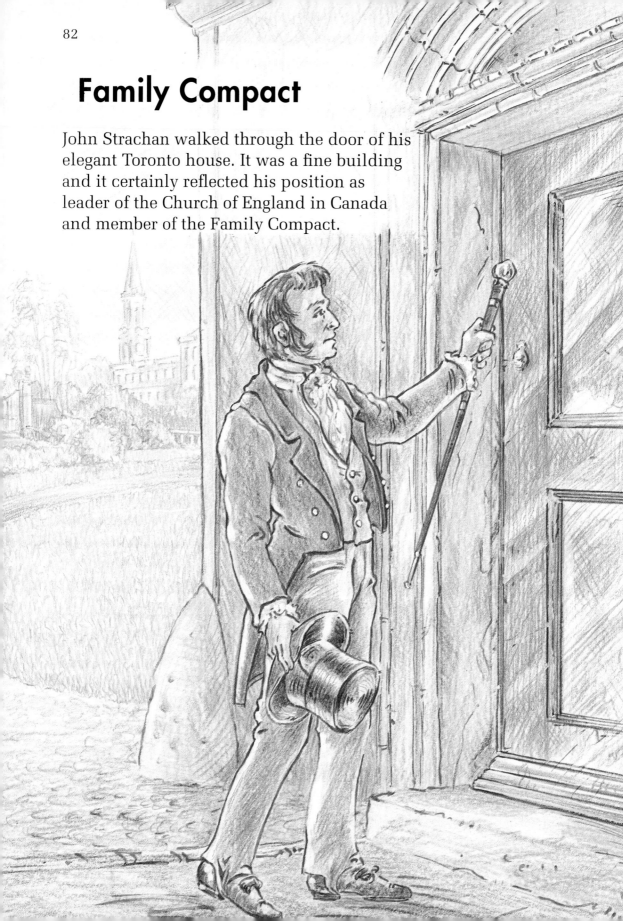

In British North America the lieutenant-governor acted as a link between the British government and the local people. He was helped in his duties as an administrator by an executive and legislative council. An elected assembly represented the colonists.

In the 1790s the governor was a powerful man, but by the 1850s his power had decreased. The power of the elected assembly had become greater, although things changed at different speeds in different colonies. In Nova Scotia, by the 1790s, the elected assembly was allowed to say how government money might be used. In the Canadas, however, the governor and his executive council controlled the money. This made them unpopular, as they had the means to do things the assembly might not want.

The executive council in Upper Canada was made up mostly of well-to-do citizens. It was dominated by a few men who came to be known as the Family Compact. They were officials who had become very close. Their families had intermarried and this created a strong bond. They were wealthy and powerful, and did not like ideas about different kinds of government. Often they were given special support by the governor.

The ordinary settlers of Upper Canada did not like being told what to do by this small group of wealthy people. They wanted more say in their government. The power of the Family Compact, as well as other issues, soon led to frustration and thoughts of rebellion.

Reform

The jostling group of young men shouted and laughed as they made their way to Toronto Bay. Some of them staggered under the weight of the printing presses they were carrying. These presses came from the offices of William Lyon Mackenzie's newspaper, the 'Colonial Advocate'. When the mob reached the edge of the bay, they grabbed boxes of type and heaved them into the water!

The mob was made up of Tories—people who supported the government in Upper Canada. They did not like the way Mackenzie was using his newspaper to criticise the government. But Mackenzie, like many people in Upper Canada, wanted change.

The reformers wanted to change the government. They wanted a shorter working day and a public health scheme to protect people against cholera. They also wanted to end the 'clergy reserves', a system that gave one-seventh of the land to the Church of England. The Church could sell or rent the land, but they charged high prices and often held on to it until prices went even higher.

This made life difficult for some settlers. Mackenzie's newspaper told people about these problems. And Mackenzie himself tried to organise a rebellion. In 1837, he and several hundred followers marched on Toronto. But the men were badly trained and the authorities quickly stopped them. Another unsuccessful rebellion occurred near Brantford. In the end, Mackenzie fled to the United States, but two of his followers were hanged, and others were banished.

'Rebellion', Lower Canada

In the early 1800s, the people of Lower Canada faced many of the same problems that existed in Upper Canada. They did not like the fact that their lieutenant-governor and his council had so much power over the elected assembly. But there was another problem to solve, and it was very complicated indeed.

In Lower Canada the lieutenant-governor was British, as were almost all of the council members. The assembly members were mostly French. The assembly had little power and was ignored by the council. The members of the assembly felt they were being looked down upon because they were French.

To make matters worse, the society in Lower Canada was dividing into groups. Rich merchants and industrialists tended to be of British background, while the only wealthy French were the seigneurs and the Catholic clergy. And they often sided with the British government. French Canadian merchants and professionals could not get government jobs.

Among working people, rivalry between British and French was made worse by immigration. Poor Irish immigrants, often carrying cholera, provided cheap labour that took jobs away from French Canadians in the cities.

Most French Canadians were farmers. New land on the seigneuries became scarce, seigneurs raised rents, and expansion into other areas of the province was blocked by British-controlled land companies. Many families did not have enough land to live off. Men had to work for other large farmers and in the lumber camps controlled by British merchants. Then in the 1830s, crop failures occurred, which caused more tension.

Reform was necessary and rebellion was inevitable. Led by reformers like Louis-Joseph Papineau, those opposed to the government began to protest even more loudly. In 1834 the assembly drew up a list of reforms called the 'Ninety-two Resolutions'. This list was rejected in 1837 by Lord Russell, the British Prime Minister, and in the same year rebellion came. A number of skirmishes took place and at St. Eustache, the patriots barricaded themselves inside the church. British troops set fire to it and almost two hundred patriots died in the flames. By the end of 1837, patriot leaders who had not been killed were in jail, in hiding, or in exile.

The British authorities had won, but now they had to resolve the problem of the colonies. They had to decide upon a new political system for the country. Now the Catholic Church was the most powerful element in French Canadian society.

Who rules?

Young Eli watched from behind a tree as his father pushed through the crowd. Eli's father was going to vote. He had to stand up in front of all these people and shout the name of the man he wanted to represent him in the assembly. When Eli's father shouted out the name, half the crowd turned toward him and booed. Some tried to push and shove him as he made his way back to the boy. Those who agreed with him cheered. This was called open voting—everyone knew who you voted for. But now that Canada had responsible government, Eli's father, like many others, wanted to do his duty—even if voting was a bit dangerous at times.

In 1838, Lord Durham was made governor-general of the Canadas. He wrote a report saying the colonies should conduct their own affairs, through an executive group or 'cabinet'. But the cabinet had to have the support of the elected assembly. This arrangement is known as 'responsible' government. It means that the cabinet members are responsible to the assembly for the policies they make. And it is the type of government Canada has now.

The British government did not agree with Durham's report immediately. But in 1841, they joined the two Canadas by an act of union. The united Canada was given an assembly, with 42 members from Canada East (Lower Canada), and 42 members from Canada West (Upper Canada). Many felt the system was unfair to French Canadians, as Canada East had a much larger population then Canada West.

In the late 1840s, the government in Britain changed its mind and sent Lord Elgin to help establish the system of responsible government. In the election of 1848 the reformers won a large majority in the assembly. Elgin asked the leaders of the Reform Party to set up a cabinet, which they did. But the cabinet had to have the support of the majority of the assembly or step down. A majority is more than half. In this way the cabinet was responsible to the assembly, which in turn was responsible to the people.

In Nova Scotia, responsible government was achieved in 1848. So, by the mid-1850s, British North America was coming close to complete self-government.

Parliament ablaze!

The mob looked angry and dangerous as it marched toward the Parliament buildings in Montreal. The members of Parliament who were still at work managed to escape as the mob broke in. Quickly the rioters began to break up the furniture, then they smashed the new gas lights. Suddenly fire broke out and the building went up in flames.

The burning of the Parliament buildings in

**Robert Baldwin
(1804–1858)**

**Louis Hippolyte LaFontaine
(1807–1864)**

Baldwin and LaFontaine led the Reform Party. Because the Reformers had more elected members in the assembly, they were called upon to make up the cabinet. The cabinet governed the country.

Montreal took place in 1849. In a way, it happened because of responsible government.

When Lord Elgin asked the Reform Party leaders, Robert Baldwin and Louis Hippolyte LaFontaine, to form a government, he was in fact giving up much of his own power. From then on, the governor would have much less authority. The cabinet and the assembly would have the real power.

One of the first things the new government did was write a proposal they wanted to become law. This proposal, called the Rebellion Losses Bill, said that people who had lost property in the rebellion of 1837 should be given money by the government to make up for their losses. Only the governor's signature was needed to make the Bill law.

Elgin signed the Bill because he knew it was what the government wanted. Before responsible government, he could have refused to sign if he had not agreed with what the Bill said.

The Rebellion Losses Bill made many people furious. They did not think rebels should be paid for rebelling. Those who disagreed most, of course, were the Tories. These were the members of the assembly and their supporters who opposed the reformers. It was a Tory mob that burned down the Parliament buildings in Montreal in protest against the Rebellion Losses Bill.

Nevertheless, the Bill became law. But it showed that responsible government could create problems as well as solve them. Montreal was never to be a political capital again. Toronto became the capital in 1850, and after that, Quebec City, then Ottawa.

Sam Slick the Clockmaker

Sam Slick showed the store keeper the marvellous clock he had for sale and explained just what a superb timepiece it was. The store keeper hummed and hawed and thought about it for a long time. It certainly was a fine clock and he felt sure he could sell it in his store. Finally he agreed to purchase Sam's clock. Sam was overjoyed. His fast talking and ingenuity had got rid of the timepiece for far more than it was worth.

Sam Slick was not a real person. He was a fictional character dreamed up in the mind of Thomas Chandler Haliburton, a Canadian humorist. Haliburton began writing humorous sketches about Sam Slick, a wandering Yankee clockmaker, in a newspaper called 'The Novascotian'. The first stories, with others added, were collected in a book called, 'The Clockmaker' or 'The Sayings and Doings of Samuel Slick of Slickville'.

In 'The Clockmaker', the Squire, who is the narrator of the story, and Sam travel through the Nova Scotia of the 1800s. Each encounter they make becomes an illustration of some political or social trait of Nova Scotians. Sam is a vain, ingenious, and smooth-talking Yankee who usually gets the better of the characters he meets and shows them up for what they really are.

Haliburton thought the Nova Scotians possessed basic British virtues, which he admired, but he thought they were failing to improve their lot by practical means, like the Yankees seemed to be doing. So Sam becomes an example for them to follow in his hard work and industry, while he represents someone to despise for his vanity and uncouth manners.

Through his stories, Haliburton was able to tell readers what he thought an ideal Nova Scotia should be. He was also able to entertain them, which makes his work enjoyable to read even today.

School days

The new boy looked around the small schoolroom. The old schoolmaster lifted a book in one hand and began to read. In the other, he held a long, thin rod. The students in the classroom listened for a while, then they began to whisper to each other. One youth started to giggle. The schoolmaster stared coldly at his pupils. Then he raised the long, thin rod and brought it crashing down on a nearby box! The students jumped. This time it had been the box—next time it might be one of them!

School life in the backwoods of British North America in the early 1800s was rough and ready. Schoolmasters were often people who could not farm or do other jobs. These men used their small cabins as schools. Often they worked in return for food or firewood. Few were good teachers.

In time, larger schools were needed. These schools, which became known as 'public schools', were set up by the government, much as they are today.

To make teaching easier, pupils in public schools were divided into grades or classes. The older children were usually taught by men; the younger children were taught by women. But soon more and more women took jobs as general teachers. Authorities said that women were better at the job, but they were often employed because they worked for less money than men. This was unfair, as women teachers did much to create the new system of education in British North America.

The Grand Trunk

The Grand Trunk railway engine chugged and puffed as smoke billowed from its huge funnel. Attached to the front was a mighty snowplough. As the engine moved forward, the sharp wedge of the snowplough drove into the snow, spraying it left and right in great white waves. Snow might delay a wagon, and ice in a river might block a boat. But engines like these could get through almost any kind of weather. This was indeed the Age of the Railway!

The first railways were built in Canada in the 1830s and ran for only short distances. The Champlain and St. Lawrence Railway between La Prairie and St. Jean covered just over 22 kilometres. But it made money for its owners.

People soon began to realise the importance of the railways. Trains could move along at between 48 and 64 kilometres per hour—a fast clip in the 1800s! They kept going during the winter months, and they usually arrived on time. In the world of transport, the railways were a giant step forward. And they helped improve commerce and industry.

In 1846, a railway was built to join Montreal to the town of Portland, Maine, in the United States. This was important to the merchants of Montreal. It meant they could transport goods to a seaport all year round.

Other railways were begun in the 1830s. But the most ambitious project, the Grand Trunk, was begun in the 1850s. This railway would run from Sarnia in Canada West to Montreal in the east, and then on to Portland, Maine.

But building a railway costs a great deal of money and soon the Grand Trunk was in financial trouble. Most of the people who had invested money in the project did not realise just how expensive it would be. So more and more money had to be raised and the governments of the provinces had to help as well.

However, by 1859 the tracks had been laid from Detroit, Michigan, in the United States to Montreal. At 1,770 kilometres, it was the longest railway in the world at that time.

Railways now began to change people's lives. Newspapers could be sent many miles away. Goods could be transported quickly, so new factories were built close to the tracks. Life seemed to move at a faster pace altogether. It would never be the same again.

Confederation

The young man looked at the cartoon. Then, with a frown, he looked at his new wife. If all the colonies in British North America were joined together, the result would probably be a stronger nation. But if the country turned out to be weak and divided, then the United States might try to take it over. That thought did not please the young man. He wanted a family, and he wanted his children to grow up in a strong, new country. Yes, he thought, confederation is the way to go after all.

In the late 1850s, people began to talk and write about confederation. It meant the joining together of the colonies of British North America under one government, though each colony would have a distinct government to look after its own affairs.

Confederation seemed a good idea for many reasons. George Brown and his Reform Party knew there were problems with the school system in Canada West. They were also unhappy about the number of seats their part of the colony had in the assembly. Canada East felt that the Union of 1841 simply was not working. But they dared not lose important trade links with the east. A confederation, with Canada divided into two separate provinces, might be the answer.

Canada West had another reason for supporting confederation. There was less and less land available to settlers. If confederation could be stretched to include the prairies, Rupert's Land, and British Columbia, more land would be available.

In Canada East, few politicians agreed with the demands of the people in Canada West. So trying to run the colony became increasingly difficult, and governments toppled quickly.

Furthermore, the American Civil War, which had begun in 1861, made people in the Canadas uneasy. They were afraid that when it ended the Americans might try to take over the British colony. This fear drew the people of British North America closer together.

Also, the railways, which were difficult and costly to build, made people look to a united land. A union of the colonies might be able to afford a railway that ran from sea to sea.

The more the people of the Canadas thought about confederation, the better the idea seemed. A nation that stretched from sea to sea would be glorious indeed!

One nation

Everywhere in British North America people were talking about union. It was an important issue—not only in the Canadas, but in the Atlantic region as well.

Many Maritimers thought a union of Nova Scotia, New Brunswick, Prince Edward Island, and Newfoundland might be a good idea. So in 1864 they prepared to hold a conference in Charlottetown. The Canadians heard of the conference and wanted to be

there too. They hoped to persuade the Maritimers to think about a union of the whole of British North America.

The conference began on September 1. The Canadians, who had arrived by ship, were very enthusiastic about their idea for a new nation. This enthusiasm was not shared by all the leaders from the Maritimes, but during the conference a plan was drawn up to make union a reality. A month later, at a second conference in Quebec, the plan was made ready to show the British government.

The British liked the plan. They tried to persuade all the colonies in British North America to agree to it quickly. But such urgency made people wary, and many began to have second thoughts.

Then, in 1866, the voters of New Brunswick showed that they really were behind the confederation movement. In Nova Scotia, however, Charles Tupper refused to hold an election on the issue because he knew he would be defeated. In fact, a group of Nova Scotians went to England and stayed there for a year to try to prevent the plan from going ahead. The group did not succeed, and on March 28, 1867, the British North America Act was signed by Queen Victoria. As of July 1, 1867, the three old colonies of Canada, Nova Scotia, and New Brunswick became the new Dominion of Canada. The Dominion had four provinces—Ontario, Quebec, Nova Scotia, and New Brunswick. Prince Edward Island and Newfoundland did not want to be part of the Dominion. But with four provinces and a great deal of hope, Canada was on its way to becoming a great new nation.

Gold rush

The miner picked up his pan and filled it with earth. Then he dipped it into the stream. Slowly he began to move the pan round in the water. As he did so, the sand and pebbles sank to the bottom, while the lighter earth escaped over the pan's sides. When all the earth was gone, the miner laid the pan in the sun to dry. The light grains of sand were blown away, leaving just pebbles—and gold dust. The miner was pleased, as there was plenty of gold dust here. He would stake his claim right away!

On April 25, 1858, the steamship 'Commodore' pulled into the harbour of Fort Victoria. On board was a group of men carrying metal pans, picks, and other tools. All of them had come for just one reason. Gold had been discovered on the Fraser River, and the British Columbia gold rush had begun.

The gold was found in gravel beds that lay along parts of the Fraser River. Water was used to wash away the gravel and separate the gold dust.

Working the gravel deposits could be dangerous. Rain and snow caused the river to rise suddenly, and the rushing water could then wash away the diggings and destroy the miners' property.

Some miners began to work among the gravel deposits away from the riverbank. But they still needed water to separate the gold. It might be pumped up or carried in wooden containers. Sometimes shafts had to be dug to get to the gold-rich gravel.

When gold was discovered in a particular area, hundreds of prospectors came. Instant towns grew up and some, like Barkerville, became quite large. But as the gold was mined out, the boom towns declined.

Few people made a lot of money from mining. But the gold rush helped to open up British Columbia.

The discovery of gold in the Fraser River region brought thousands of fortune hunters into the territory.

Boom towns sprang up during the gold rush.

The National Policy

The farmer proudly stroked his new harvester. It looked as if it would do the job all right. And not only that, it had been made in Canada! The farmer might have bought an American machine. But now—because of John A. Macdonald's National Policy—American goods were often more expensive. The 'policy' protected goods made in Canada by putting a heavy tax on foreign items.

Manufacturers in Canada wanted to sell their products in their own home market. But imported products, especially those from the United States, were often cheaper. Many American manufacturers used Canada to get rid of goods they could not sell at home. Sometimes, they just wanted to dump the goods, and they didn't even care if they made a profit.

Canadian manufacturers did not like this. They wanted protection. And they could have that protection if the government were to put high taxes on imported goods. The National Policy, drawn up in 1879, did just that. It also supported the building of railways and encouraged people to emigrate to Canada.

Not everybody liked the National Policy, though. It did help manufacturers and labourers, but mostly in the industrial areas around Toronto and Montreal, where huge factories grew up. But the smaller businesses in the Maritimes could not compete. Some small cotton, sugar, and woollen mills had to close. They were bought by larger companies. Also, local farmers could not sell their wheat as cheaply as farmers in western Canada, so they had difficulties, too.

The National Policy increased the cost of some things, such as furniture, woollen clothing, and cotton goods. And some Americans avoided the heavy import taxes by building branch factories in Canada. These factories employed Canadians, but they were owned by Americans. Clearly, the National Policy helped some—but not all—people.

Rebellion in the northwest

The trial was over. The decision had been made. Louis Riel was found guilty of treason and sentenced to death. On November 16, 1885, the métis leader was hanged at Regina.

Louis Riel was born in 1844. His father was métis, his mother French-Canadian. The métis were mostly descendants of the French or British fur traders and Indian women. They lived on the prairies and in spring and summer did a little farming, but they were best known as fearless and skilled buffalo hunters. A métis hunter could bring down an animal from as far away as 90 metres!

The métis were unhappy about Canadians in the east interfering in their lives. They were afraid they would lose their land and their way of life. Riel knew the problems of his people and he became their leader. In 1869, he and his men formed a provisional government at Lower Fort Garry, the Hudson's Bay Company's centre at the forks of the Red and Assiniboine rivers. They refused to recognise the governor sent from Canada and wanted the Canadian government to agree to discuss their problems. This convinced the government to create the province of Manitoba, where the métis and the French would have special rights.

Louis Riel had succeeded in getting much of what he wanted, but his methods had angered many people in Canada. And when a métis court sentenced Thomas Scott, a troublemaker from Ontario, to death, their anger grew. Soldiers were sent to Manitoba and Riel was forced into hiding. He was banished from Canada for five years.

In the early 1880s, the métis and native peoples of Saskatchewan faced the same problems as their brothers had done in Manitoba. They brought Louis Riel back from the United States to lead the rebellion of 1885. The rebellion failed. Riel was captured and hanged for treason.

His death pleased many Canadians, but it angered many others. Some considered Riel a hero; others called him a traitor. Even today, historians do not agree which of these Louis Riel actually was.

Canada First

Charles Mair sat at his desk and tried to finish the poem he was working on. But he could not concentrate. Instead, his imagination kept turning to the wonders of the Canadian west, which he longed to visit. He could imagine the Dominion of Canada stretching across the continent of North America. One day, of course, his dream would be a reality.

Charles Mair was born in 1838 in the town of Lanark, Upper Canada. He wanted to be a doctor, and attended Queen's University for a time. But he did not earn his degree. Instead he grew to love and write poetry.

In 1869, he went to Ottawa to become a

journalist. There he met members of the 'Canada First' movement. The Canada Firsters, such as Henry J. Morgan, George T. Denison, and Robert G. Haliburton, shared Charles' views on the west. They especially liked the idea of the Red River becoming part of Canada.

When Charles was given the opportunity to work in the Red River area, he was delighted. He sent letters from Red River to the 'Globe' newspaper in Toronto. But his articles about the métis and Red River were often offensive. He showed that he did not fully understand the problems involved. Eventually, after Louis Riel threatened to execute him, Charles fled to Ontario.

But Charles could not resist the west and he soon returned. As time passed, he gained a better understanding of the métis people. In 1886, he published a verse play called 'Tecumseh: a Drama'. This play showed Charles' patriotism and his understanding of native peoples.

Charles and other writers, like W. A. Foster, tried to express the hope of the Canada First movement both in politics and culture. They wanted to see a new nationality grow and to see Canada as a great united country. Their thoughts inspired magazines such as the 'Nation' and 'Canadian Monthly'. In turn, the magazines helped Canada form its culture. They gave new writers a chance to be read.

The Canada First movement did not last long. But it helped the development of Canadian arts—from the journalism of the early days to the golden age of Canadian lyric poetry in the 1880s.

The Canadian Pacific

In 1871, Sir John A. Macdonald, prime minister of Canada, told the people of British Columbia that if they would agree to confederation he would build a railway to the Pacific by 1881. Many people supported this idea. After all, it took months to travel from the east to the Pacific by canoe, horse, or wagon. A railway would unite the country. And it would stop the prairie settlements and perhaps even British Columbia from falling into the grasping hands of the United States of America!

But others laughed. Building a railway would be far too difficult, they reasoned. The mountains were too high, the passes too

The Canadian Pacific was Canada's first transcontinental railway.

dangerous, and the swamps too risky! Then in 1873 a scandal erupted. Macdonald had taken money from Sir Hugh Allen to help pay for his 1872 election. Macdonald was accused of giving the Pacific Railway contract to Allen's company in return. The Liberals got hold of all the documents that told of the deal. The government was defeated in the next election. The new prime minister—Alexander Mackenzie—was not interested in building railways quickly. So, in 1878, when Macdonald returned to power, British Columbia was still without its promised railway.

The government had to act, but it now knew the project was too expensive for the government to do alone. Help was needed. So a group of businessmen banded together to put money into the railway. They were known as the 'Syndicate'. They later became the Canadian Pacific Railway Company.

At last the job ended. On November 7, 1885, the last spike was driven home. The Canadian Pacific Railway was completed.

The North-West Mounted Police

Two bearded men slouched against the wooden boxes stacked along the wall in the tiny hut. One man grabbed a box and pulled out a bottle of golden liquid. Suddenly, there was a knock at the door. Startled, the man dropped the bottle. The second man reached for his gun. As he did so, two figures in bright scarlet coats rushed in. "Throw down your weapons!" ordered one of the uniformed men. "You are under arrest!" The two whiskey smugglers did as they were told. They did not wish to argue with the North-West Mounted Police.

The North-West Mounted Police were formed in 1873 to fight lawlessness in western Canada. Their special tasks were to stop the illegal trade in whiskey, to keep the peace between settlers and native peoples, and to collect taxes due on alcohol and other goods.

The North-West Mounted Police were like a combination of soldiers and policemen. They could catch criminals and they could also put them on trial. This seemed like a lot of power for one group. But the Mounties, as they came to be known, were very successful and did not abuse their powers.

Today the force is called the Royal Canadian Mounted Police. They no longer try criminals. However, their record for law enforcement is very good, and their fame has spread throughout the world.

Canada's first woman doctor

A young woman walked into the doctor's consulting room. Normally she would be nervous about seeing a doctor, but today she smiled. She felt relaxed. Her new doctor was Emily Stowe, the first woman doctor in Canada.

Emily Howard Stowe was born in 1831 in the community of South Norwich, Upper Canada. She was educated at Toronto Normal School and at the age of 15 became a teacher.

During her years as a teacher, Emily began to think about becoming a doctor. She thought it was wrong that only men could be doctors. She knew that women often found it difficult to visit a male doctor and felt sure they would feel better about visiting a female one.

Then, when Emily's husband fell ill with tuberculosis, she made up her mind to do something. She decided to become a doctor. But when she tried to become a student at a Canadian medical school, she was refused admission!

Emily did not give up, though. She went to the United States, where she was accepted by the New York Medical College for Women. Emily studied there for many years until, in 1867, she became the first Canadian woman to receive a degree in medicine.

Emily returned to Canada, but still she was not allowed to work as a doctor. Bravely, she fought for her rights. Finally, in 1880, she was licensed to practice medicine. She went on to become a successful doctor in Toronto.

Emily continued to fight for women's rights. She believed that women should be given the chance to go to university and the right to vote. She helped establish the Women's Medical College in Toronto in 1883 and founded the Women's Literary Club, which worked for women's suffrage. She began the Dominion Women's Enfranchisement Association, which also worked to help women get the vote. Emily died in 1903.

Winnipeg

Trams and wagons rattled along the busy
street. People walked on wooden sidewalks
that kept some of the dust away from their
feet. Everyone looked energetic and eager.
Winnipeg was an important town now—the
business centre of the prairies.

    Before white people came, Cree and
Assiniboine peoples lived in the area that is

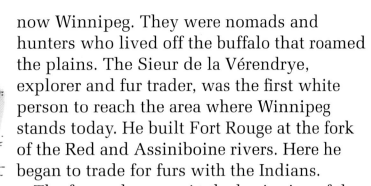

now Winnipeg. They were nomads and hunters who lived off the buffalo that roamed the plains. The Sieur de la Vérendrye, explorer and fur trader, was the first white person to reach the area where Winnipeg stands today. He built Fort Rouge at the fork of the Red and Assiniboine rivers. Here he began to trade for furs with the Indians.

The fur trade grew. At the beginning of the 1800s, the North West Company and the Hudson's Bay Company battled for control of the trade in this area. Meanwhile, the Earl of Selkirk sent Scottish Highlanders to settle there. The settlement was later called the Red River Settlement and Scots, along with Irish and others, lived and worked there. The settlement grew and prospered.

In time the Hudson's Bay Company lands were sold to the Dominion of Canada. This, along with the pressure put on the government by métis leader Louis Riel, led to the founding of a new province called Manitoba in 1870. That same year, the Red River Settlement was renamed Winnipeg and became the capital of the province. At that time Winnipeg had a population of around 1,900.

Winnipeg was well placed, and in 1878, it was linked by rail to St. Paul in the United States. In 1881, the building of the Canadian Pacific Railway connected it to eastern Canada. So Winnipeg became a gateway to the west and to the east. Its trade grew, like the city itself. More people came to the west from other countries in the late 1800s and early 1900s. They also helped Winnipeg grow and prosper.

Can you hear me?

Alexander Graham Bell frowned as he looked down at his clothes. What a mess! He had spilled battery acid. He needed help from his colleague, who was in the next room. "Mr. Watson, come here, I want you!" he demanded.

Mr. Watson could hardly believe his ears. The words he heard had not come through the door or through the wall. Instead they had come from the transmitter of Bell's new invention—the telephone!

For years, Alexander Graham Bell had been trying to find a way of carrying voice sounds by electricity. So far, he had been able to transmit sounds but not words. At last, on March 10, 1876, the first understandable sentence had been carried on wire by electricity.

Bell exhibited his telephones later that year at the Centennial Exhibition in Philadelphia. The Bell Telephone Company, the first telephone company in the United States, began operations on July 9, 1877.

Alexander Bell was born in 1847 in Scotland. While he was still young he became very interested in helping the deaf. His father, Alexander Melville Bell, taught the deaf and wrote books on how to speak correctly. Alexander Graham also became a teacher. Then he began to help his father with voice training. In 1870 the Bells moved to Brantford in Ontario. From there, Alexander went to Boston, where he carried out many of his experiments with sound and electricity. He also lived for much of his life in the town of Baddeck, Nova Scotia.

He worked on many different things, including photoelectric cells, super sheep, hydrofoil boats, and aircraft. His 'Silver Dart' was the first plane to fly in Canada.

Alexander Graham Bell is perhaps Canada's best-known inventor. But he wanted to be known only as a teacher of the deaf.

Inuit soapstone carvings were originally made for religious purposes. Now they are appreciated as works of art.

People of the snow

The Inuit father looked carefully at the piece of soft soapstone. Just a little more work, he thought, and the job would be done. He began to carve again, moulding the soapstone into

the shape of a smooth grey seal. Soon he would be able to give it to his son. It would bring the boy luck in the seal hunt.

The Inuit people live in the far north of Canada. They are hunters and fishermen, but they are also skilled craftsmen. They carve ivory into buttons and buckles shaped like animals. They also decorate weapons and tools and make beautiful objects from the soft rock called soapstone.

The Inuit way of life is very old. The ancestors of the Inuit probably crossed from northeast Asia to Alaska about 10,000 years ago. In order to live, the Inuit hunted mostly seals and caribou. But they also killed musk oxen, polar bears, whales, and some birds. They used harpoons with bone or stone tips to kill seals. Caribou were hunted in summer and fall. The women often helped hunt the animals by chasing the herd toward the men, who remained hidden, ready to attack with spears.

Caribou and other animal skins were used to make clothes and tents. Skins were also used to build the Inuit canoes, called kayaks.

In summer, Inuit families lived in skin tents or sometimes in sod houses. In winter, many families built snow houses, either as temporary shelters or permanent homes.

The Inuit followed their traditional way of life until the 1880s. But then the growth of the whaling industry brought European ships into the dangerous Arctic waters where they met the Inuit hunters. At the same time the northward expansion of the fur trade brought people from the south. Slowly the Inuit began to change their ways.

Canada's breadbasket

The immigrant farmer had picked the best place on his new land to build a house. He had little money to spend so he decided to build a sod house. It would cost very little.

First the farmer cut pieces of sod from the ground. Each piece was about 1 metre long and 25 centimetres wide. He hauled the sod to the site for his house. Already he had dug trenches for the four walls. Carefully, he arranged the sod, like bricks, to make a double wall. He left an opening for the door, and cut holes where he wanted windows. When the walls were finished, he placed poplar poles across the tops from wall to wall and arranged sod and hay on the poles to make a roof.

Once the house was built, farming could begin. But in the west, summers were dry and short, and farming was not easy. So wheat became the main crop.

A man called David Fife, who lived in Ontario, developed a special wheat for Canada. He planted wheat seeds from Scotland, which produced only a few stalks but with good large heads. The following year, he sowed the seeds from these stalks. In time, he developed the hardy wheat now called Red Fife.

Many people travelled west to try farming. Some came from Britain and the United States, others from eastern European countries such as Russia and Poland. Eastern Europeans were thought to adapt best to life in the Canadian west. But they often had problems because they were so poor and they spoke neither English nor French.

Some could not stand the hardships. They went home or drifted into towns to try to find easier work. But those who stayed helped build the west into Canada's breadbasket.

Many immigrants to the prairies built sod houses. These modest homes provided shelter until something better could be built.

Nellie McClung

The crowd leaned forward on their seats, anxious not to miss a word. The woman on the stage had been talking for some time now, and it was clear why she was so popular on the lecture circuit. She was a very good speaker indeed. Her topic was the evils of drink and she made anyone who touched a drop of alcohol fairly quake with guilt. The lady was Nellie McClung and her motto was "never retract, never explain and never apologise!" She was certainly a woman who knew her own mind.

THE EVIL OF DRINK

Nellie was born in Chatsworth, Ontario, the daughter of a farmer. Then in the 1880s the family moved west and began farming in the Souris Valley near Brandon, Manitoba. Nellie knew that she wanted to do something useful with her life, so she attended Winnipeg Normal School and graduated as a teacher. It was the only profession a woman could enter in those years. But when she married Robert Wesley McClung, she gave up teaching and became a housewife.

Her sharp mind needed something to occupy it, though, and in 1907 Nellie became inspired by the fight against the evils of drink. She joined the Women's Christian Temperance Society and spoke out in favour of the prohibition of alcohol in Canada. Prohibition meant that alcohol simply could not be sold. She felt this was the only way to stop drunkenness and the unhappiness it caused the families of heavy drinkers.

Nellie also began to fight for the rights of women. She joined the Political Equity League, a group that argued for the right of women across Canada to have the vote.

But Nellie did not stop there. She was the first woman chosen to attend a Methodist World Congress, and she was appointed to the first Board of Governors of the Canadian Broadcasting Company. She was a member of the Canadian delegation to the League of Nations in 1938 and still found time to write books and novels about her own life!

Nellie McClung died in 1951. She was an untiring reformer and fought hard for worthy causes. She was known as the "Holy Terror" and Nellie lived up to her nickname.

Lucy Maud of Green Gables

Lucy Maud thought hard. She needed a plot for a serial she was to write for a newspaper. While she was thinking, she happened to glance at a newspaper clipping she had put aside. The heading was rather odd. It read: 'Elderly couple apply to orphan asylum for a boy; by mistake a girl is sent to them'. Lucy Maud smiled. She need look no further. Here was a wonderful plot for a story. And it was even better because Lucy Maud herself had been an orphan. But she did not want to waste such a good plot on a serial. It would have to be a book. So, from that clipping, 'Anne of Green Gables' was born.

'Anne of Green Gables' was Lucy Maud Montgomery's first book. It tells about childhood on a farm on Prince Edward Island in the late 1800s. In the book, the author paints a very clear picture of what it was like to live in those times. 'Anne of Green Gables' was a tremendous success, partly because Lucy Maud used her own childhood experiences on Prince Edward Island to make it come alive. The book is still widely read and has been made into plays for the stage and for television.

Lucy Maud was born in 1874 at Clifton on Prince Edward Island. Her mother died when Lucy Maud was very young, so she went to live with her grandparents on a farm, where she learned about country life.

Lucy Maud loved to read and she began writing poems when she was a teenager. Later she trained as a teacher, but writing was her first love. She sold her first piece of work, a short story, while she was still in college. She was paid $5!

In 1901 she joined the staff of the 'Daily Echo', a Halifax newspaper. But when her grandmother became ill, Lucy gave up her job and moved back to Cavendish to look after her. She taught at the local school but she continued to write. She wrote mostly poems and short stories for American magazines. Then came 'Anne of Green Gables'.

Lucy Maud Montgomery wrote many books after this, including six others about Anne. They were all popular, but none became so well loved as 'Anne of Green Gables'.

Imperial connections

The battle was hard and bloody, but the men of the 2nd Royal Canadian Regiment fought bravely, and many felt that victory was close at hand. Their enemy, the Boers of South Africa, had defended their position at Paardeberg as best they could. But the troops of the British Empire were stronger, and on February 27, 1900, the battle ended.

The Battle of Paardeberg took place during the South African War, or Boer War, which began in 1899 and ended in 1902. The Boers were descendants of Dutch farmers who had settled in South Africa years earlier. The war began when the British decided to take over the Orange Free State and the South African Republic (now Transvaal), the two Boer states in southern Africa. Britain wanted all of South Africa to be part of the British Empire, which then included Canada, Australia, and other countries. Britain was interested in the riches to be found there, as well as in enlarging the Empire. Britain also felt that soldiers from countries in the Empire should help in the fight.

Many Canadians disagreed with what Britain was doing in South Africa. Some thought the Boer republics had the right to develop on their own. Other Canadians supported the English-speaking people in South Africa and wanted to see the Empire grow. Those who supported the Empire were called 'Imperialists'.

Canada's Prime Minister, Wilfrid Laurier, listened to both points of view. He knew that many French Canadians did not support

The Battle of Paardeberg was the first victory for the first Canadian troops to serve in a country other than their own.

the war because they felt the Boers were in a similar position to their own, a non-English-speaking people in an English-speaking Empire. But he also knew that many English-speaking Canadians supported Britain's imperialist ideas.

In the end, Laurier decided to send troops, but stipulated that they had to be volunteers. So the first soldiers set sail from Quebec in

1899. In all, more than 7,000 Canadian troops served in South Africa.

The South African War made many Canadians think about their role in the British Empire. Some thought Canada ought to strengthen the Empire and protect it through defence and trade policies. Others wanted less control by Britain. They felt Canada should be allowed more freedom to grow and develop on its own.

Canada at war

Before 1914, few Canadians had worried about a world war. Now Canada, as part of a world community, had to accept a new role. When World War I began, most Canadians supported the British cause. But few knew how horrible the war would be.

In 1915, the first Canadians arrived in France. Many more followed in the next few years. Most were soldiers, but some joined the Royal Flying Corps and became airmen. The airmen flew light planes, and their daring and courage in the air soon became legendary.

But it was Canada's army that did so much to help the cause. In 1916, the Canadian Corps fought bravely at the Battle of the Somme in France. Canadians also fought at Passchendaele, Belgium, and at Vimy Ridge, France. Today a war memorial dedicated to these Canadian soldiers stands at the top of the ridge. In all, 600,000 Canadian men served in World War I and 60,000 died.

While the war continued, Canadians at home did their part. Canada's farms and farmers became very important to the war effort. Wheat, flour, meat, and cattle were sent to Europe to help feed the people. Wood and metals were sent to build machines. And industry in Canada grew as more and more guns and shells were needed.

In 1918, the war ended and Canada proudly took its place among the victorious nations.

But all was not well at home. During the war, both French- and English-speaking Canadians enlisted in the armed forces. But the French Canadians—having no enthusiasm for either the British or French cause—sent fewer men, and English Canadians resented this. They did not understand that French Canadians felt differently about British imperialism. Both sides mistrusted each other. The problem of race became important again. Canada was united in some ways but not yet in others.

On strike!

The horses' hooves clattered as the police rode hard down North Main Street. Then the murmur of men's voices rose to drown out the sound. Mounted police and strikers met and neither would give way. Some men were hurt in the fighting. One was shot.

That eventful day became known as Bloody Saturday. It was June 21, 1919—the beginning of the end of the Winnipeg general strike!

When World War I ended, many people in Canada felt let down. The 'better Canada' they had been promised did not seem to exist. Many soldiers who returned from the war found jobs, but others did not. And some of the people who had jobs felt they should have higher wages and better working conditions. They believed that workers should band together to support each other. In some cases they formed unions.

Unions had existed in Canada for some time, but many workers in the west wanted one large union. Workers had also heard about the Russian Revolution—a revolution of the working people against their bosses and rulers. This made Canadian workers even more determined to change their situation.

In Winnipeg, the workers went on strike when the employers of the building and metal trade workers refused to recognise their union. The employers did not want their employees to be able to make demands as a large group. Instead they wanted to deal only with men who worked directly for their company.

By mid-May, 70 unions, including the streetcar drivers and postal workers, had joined in the strike. Those who disagreed with the strikers called them 'revolutionaries'. A citizens' committee was formed to fight the strikers. The government threatened the strikers with the loss of their jobs. Laws were then passed to close down certain organisations. The police and the army were on standby. Strike leaders were arrested and riots broke out, during which one striker was killed and 30 injured. By the end of June the strike was over and the unions were forced to give in.

The Winnipeg general strike showed how strong workers can be when they band together. But it also showed that the state was powerful enough to use the law and its armed forces to maintain its authority.

The Group of Seven

Men and women wandered around the art gallery looking at the paintings that hung on the wall. Some liked what they saw. Others did not understand what the seven artists on display were trying to do. They thought the colours too violent and the outlines too bold.

But soon many of these people would come to recognise the work of the artists—now known as the 'Group of Seven'—as the most exciting paintings of Canadian nature and landscape they had seen. The paintings made you feel how vast and colourful the country was, and how harsh the climate could be. The work of the Group of Seven was truly Canadian.

The Group of Seven included A. Y. Jackson, Lawren Harris, Frederick H. Varley, Franz Johnston, Arthur Lismer, J. E. H. MacDonald, and Franklin Carmichael. This group of painters felt that Canada—a young and robust country—needed a similar kind of art. They visited places with rugged landscapes, such as Georgian Bay, Algonquin Park, and Algoma. The group painted scenery in a way they felt showed the true spirit of Canada. They did not like the industrialised society of the cities and so did not paint city scenes.

One other artist—Tom Thomson—was important to the seven. Thomson is often considered to be one of the group, as he influenced some of its members and felt much as they did about painting. Unfortunately Thomson drowned in 1917, three years before the group's exhibition.

'Algoma, November' is one of many Canadian wilderness landscapes painted by A. Y. Jackson.

"The Elements' depicts a storm forming over Georgian Bay. It shows the bold lines and brilliant colours J. E. H. MacDonald traditionally used.

On to Ottawa!

The young man walked slowly along the empty train track, stepping on each wooden sleeper. When he reached the ribbon of freight cars standing fixed on the opposite line, he moved across. Now there were other men with him, talking in low voices. Some walked farther along the line. Others began to climb onto the freight cars. The young man joined them. He would 'ride the rods' to Ottawa. He would join the others in protest against unemployment and the bad times.

This was Canada in the 1930s—the time of the Great Depression. In the 1920s all had seemed well. Then, in 1929, the New York stock market crashed. Trade, manufacturing, and farming all began to suffer. By the mid-1930s, things had not changed. People were not investing their money in industry. Markets for goods and food were getting smaller. To make matters worse, the summers were hot and dry. Rich topsoil was blown away and crops failed.

As unemployment rose, people grew angry. They felt the government should do something to help. Many asked for financial help called 'relief' from the government, and some lived in relief camps. Life in these camps was discouraging and, in 1935, some men from camps in the west rebelled. They decided to 'trek' to Ottawa by rail. But the trekkers were stopped at Regina, where there was rioting and bloodshed.

During the 1930s, different governments tried to weather the storm but it seemed impossible. By the end of the decade some progress had been made. But it was a startling new danger that created the change—World War II broke out in 1939. The government had to create more jobs and spend more money. One tragedy helped to end another.

Canada broadcasting

"He shoots, he scores!" These famous words became known all over Canada when Foster Hewitt voiced the play-by-play of National Hockey League games. Foster acquired many thousands of devoted fans who listened eagerly to his 'Hockey Night in Canada' programme. And it was brought to them by the Canadian Broadcasting Corporation.

The Canadian Broadcasting Corporation, or CBC as it is more commonly known, first went on the air in 1936. However, the first radio programme in Canada was actually broadcast from Montreal in 1920. During the 1920s, many private radio stations were set up. Some were connected with newspapers; others were linked to religious groups. Many Canadians tuned in to stations in the United States as well, and this worried certain people in the government, who thought that the American influence might be harmful. So a committee was set up to look carefully at how radio stations were licensed and owned. Their report said that Canada should have a publicly owned system modelled on the British Broadcasting Corporation. It should provide coverage to all settled parts of the country and develop Canadian programmes. Funding should come from a license fee on all radio sets.

The Canadian Broadcasting Corporation, with both French and English networks, was soon established. The CBC helped to promote culture and provide many Canadians with a more educated outlook on national and international affairs.

In 1952, the CBC began transmitting television programmes. Although some of the most popular ones from the United States were shown and commercials were used, the CBC devoted much energy to the production of Canadian drama and music and the development of shows on current affairs. Sporting events were very popular as well, and now 'Hockey Night in Canada' could be seen as well as heard.

War again

The grey boats cut through the oily water. One after the other they came into Bedford Basin. Men and machines, food and wood were loaded onto the boats that did not yet have a cargo. When they were all full and in position, the boats set off. The great convoy was bound for Europe—and a raging war.

In September 1939, Britain had declared war on Nazi Germany. Canada, no longer a colony in the British Empire, but an independent country in the British Commonwealth, joined Britain a week later. And it declared war on Japan in December of 1941.

The Canadian Navy helped escort large convoys of ships across the Atlantic Ocean from Canada to Europe. The convoys carried men, arms, and food, and they were constantly pursued by German submarines called U-boats. By 1945 and the end of the war, the Canadian Navy was the third largest in the world.

The Royal Canadian Air Force—third in size among Western allies—fought in Europe, and played an equally important role in the training of pilots. Thousands of men came to Canada to learn to fly.

The Canadian Army also did much to help the war effort, playing an important role from D-Day to the end of the conflict. Canadians were part of the bitter march through Italy, which ended with the fall of Rome. They also participated in the Allied landing at Normandy in France.

The Canadian government lent billions of dollars to the war cause. It sent the British people large quantities of food during the Battle of Britain, Canadian factories built thousands of planes, ships, and weapons.

By the end of the war, more than a million Canadian men and women had served in the armed forces. More than 90,000 had been killed or wounded.

At home, the years of the Great Depression were over. Canada became an important exporter again, and few people were unemployed. In 1940, a new system of unemployment insurance saw the birth of a Canadian social security system. In 1944, it adopted a program that assisted families by providing financial aid for children. By the end of the war, despite all the hardships people had suffered, Canada was about to enter a new era of prosperity.

Bush pilot

The small aircraft banked steeply to the left, then straightened out and flew inland. The country below was rocky and barren. It was also hundreds of kilometres from civilization. If anything happened to the plane, the pilot would be in real trouble. It took great courage to fly over the bleak north country. Pilot 'Punch' Dickens had that courage, and he also had the skill. Punch was a great bush pilot.

Clennell H. ('Punch') Dickens

Punch was born at Portage la Prairie in 1899. His real name was Clennell H. Dickens. He joined the Royal Flying Corps when he was 18 and won the Distinguished Flying Cross for his exploits in World War I. In 1924, he joined the Royal Canadian Air Force and gained much experience flying in Canada. He left the air force in 1927.

A year later, two American mining men asked Punch to go on a flight that would carry him far into the north. The flight would be long and dangerous, but Punch knew he could do it. He would fly almost 5,000 kilometres, from Winnipeg to Hudson's Bay and Chesterfield Inlet, then west to Thelon River and southwest to Fort Smith.

The flight took 27 hours. The journey would have taken a year by ordinary Arctic transport.

The era of the bush pilots began in the late 1920s. Bush pilots were willing to fly anywhere in the north. They took tremendous risks and not all of them survived. Their planes had no modern direction-finding devices, and pilots often flew without radio contact. But their daring helped change the lives of people living in the north. Instead of being months away from the nearest cities, they were just days away. This helped greatly in rescue situations and benefited people with health problems.

New Canadians

The New Canadians stood proudly. They had come to the Citizenship Court to receive the papers that would make them true citizens of Canada. There were people from many parts

of Europe, including Italy, Poland, and England, as well as Asian people from India, Hong Kong, and Korea.

At the end of the ceremony, the new citizens talked among themselves. They told stories of how they came to be in Canada and said how much they appreciated living in their new country.

In the 1930s, unemployment had forced the government to restrict immigration into Canada. But World War II seemed to create jobs for everyone, so immigration picked up again. During the war, many British women married Canadian soldiers. Later, they travelled to Canada with their children. These 'war brides' began a new wave of immigration.

After World War II, Prime Minister Mackenzie King announced a new immigration policy. No longer were distinctions to be made between 'acceptable' northern Europeans and 'unacceptable' southern Europeans. Full citizenship was given to Asian Canadians, and human rights codes were passed in Saskatchewan and Ontario to end the discrimination against blacks, Jews, and Canadian native peoples.

Most Canadians accepted this flood of immigrants because there were plenty of jobs and because immigrants were willing to take jobs that many other Canadians didn't want. Between 1945 and 1951, more than 500,000 new citizens began new lives in Canada.

What does Quebec want?

A group of Quebec nationalists walked proudly down the street. It was 1976 and they were jubilant because the Parti Québécois had been elected to office in their province. Many now believed Quebec would become a nation in its own right.

In the years after World War II, Quebec began to change. The people of Quebec became more sure of themselves. They

wanted much more control over their society. At the same time, people outside the province began to take more interest in Quebec's art, music, and literature. Also, the Labour movement grew in strength, the role of women started to change, and families became smaller. All these things clearly showed that a new kind of society was developing in the province.

In the 1960s, during what was known as the 'Quiet Revolution', education, social policy, and health care were reformed and modernised. But many Québécois wanted more say in their government. The idea of Quebec as a separate state began to take hold in many people's minds.

In 1963, the Front de Libération du Québec, or FLQ, was formed. Its aim was to organise an uprising by the people. The FLQ believed that they could not get what they wanted through peaceful means. So they turned to violence. In 1970, FLQ men and women kidnapped and killed Pierre Laporte, the Quebec Minister of Labour. The government applied the War Measures Act, and the army was sent to Montreal. More than 400 FLQ sympathisers were arrested.

The Parti Québécois, however, hoped to secure independence by peaceful means—if independence was what the people wanted. So on May 20, 1980, they held a 'referendum', or public vote, to see if the people of Quebec really wanted an independent state. But only 40 per cent of the people voted for independence. The people proved to be less keen on change than the Parti had hoped.

Yet the independence question persisted. In 1994, legislative elections were held in Quebec, and the Parti Québécois won the majority of seats. Its leader, Jacques Parizeau, became premier. The new government pledged to work for provincial independence and economic development.

A Sporting Nation

Long before Europeans came to Canada, the native peoples enjoyed the hard and exciting game now called lacrosse. Sometimes huge teams of nearly 1,000 warriors competed against each other. Today, although the teams are much smaller, the game is still tough and demanding. Players like John Tavares and twins Paul and Gary Gait have made lacrosse a great spectator sport.

Canada's national game, however, is not lacrosse but ice-hockey, perhaps the fastest team sport in the world. Young players can join amateur teams when they are 7 years old or younger.

Isabel Brasseur and Lloyd Eisler won a silver medal at the 1994 Winter Olympics.

Downhill skier Kerrin Lee-Gartner won a gold medal at the 1992 Winter Olympics.

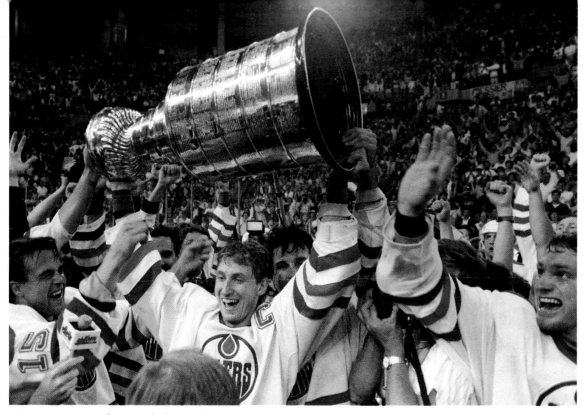

Wayne Gretzky and the Edmonton Oilers took
home the Stanley Cup in 1987.

From there they may go on to
play in North America's top
professional league, the National
Hockey League. NHL teams are
based in the United States as well
as Canada, but most of the players
are Canadian. 'Rocket' Richard is
one of the all-time greats of the
game, and Wayne Gretzky has
become the finest player of the
modern era.

Football is played during the
autumn months, both at
university and professional
levels. Canadian football's rules
are slightly different than those of
American football, but the game
is just as entertaining. Great
Canadian football stars include
Peter Dalla Riva and Lui Passaglia.

Professional baseball came to
Canada in 1969. Now both
Montreal and Toronto boast
teams. Roberto Alomar made his
name with the Bluejays, while
Moises Alou thrilled crowds with
the Montreal Expos.

Canadians have always done
well at winter sports, especially
downhill ski races and ice
skating. Kerrin Lee-Gartner is a
gold-medal-winning downhill
skier. And Canadian skating duo
Isabel Brasseur and Lloyd
Eisler have won numerous
medals and championships.

Giving back the land

The Lubicon chief stood beside the blockade checkpoint. Overhead a Royal Canadian Mounted Police plane circled, while several mounties set up a station 1 kilometre from the blockade. About 200 Lubicon Indians and supporters had gathered at the checkpoint to prevent anyone from driving into land they claimed was theirs!

The blockade was set up around Lubicon Lake, Alberta—traditional hunting and fishing grounds of the native peoples. The Lubicons felt they should have been granted that land in the 1800s when treaties with other Indians were made, but they had been overlooked. For many years the Lubicons had tried unsuccessfully to have the land declared a reserve.

Then in the 1950s the oil men came. Again a treaty was requested and the government refused to listen. By the 1980s, roads had been bulldozed and pipelines laid, nearly destroying the traditional way of life.

In 1984 the Canadian government finally offered the Indians 65.7 square kilometres of land but the Indians wanted at least 233 square kilometres.

In 1988, the Lubicons blocked the roads that led into the land. After arrests had been made, the premier of Alberta agreed to re-open talks with the Indians. At last an agreement was made—the Lubicons would receive 245 square kilometres of land if the federal government agreed.

Many groups and individuals had supported the Lubicons. Their peaceful protest had worked.

The landslide

Kim Campbell, Canada's first female prime minister, took the oath of office in 1993.

The old Tory stared at the newspaper in disbelief. "How could this have happened?" he muttered under his breath as he read the election results. It was a disaster for the Conservative Party, a landslide defeat at the hands of the Liberals! Still, he had to admit that Brian Mulroney had been one of the least popular prime ministers in Canadian history and that he had not expected Mulroney's successor, Kim Campbell, to be reelected. But this! This was a defeat beyond the worst Tory nightmare.

Many other dyed-in-the-wool Tories may have felt the same way after the Canadian election of 1993. Mulroney had resigned in June of that year, causing some people to dislike him even more for walking out when he knew he would not last. His place was taken by Kim Campbell, who became the first female Canadian prime minister. Some thought Campbell would become a sort of Canadian Margaret Thatcher, the British prime minister known as the 'Iron Lady'. But others rightly believed she was a scapegoat prime minister, who would have to suffer defeat instead of Mulroney.

When the field was set for the election battle, the Conservatives held 154 seats in the House of Commons, while the Liberals held just 79. But after the election votes had been counted, the statistics were much different. The Liberals, lead by Jean Chrétien, now held 177 seats, a gain of nearly 100, and were ahead of the Conservatives. The

Conservatives lost all but a shocking two seats! This opened the door for two fairly new regional parties to become the second and third most powerful parties in the land. One, the Bloc Québécois, became the official opposition, with 54 seats. It was founded in 1990, and its members would like to see Quebec become a separate country from Canada. The third-largest party, with 52 seats, is the Alberta-based Reform Party.

A confident Jean Chrétien campaigned in Winnipeg in 1993 for the post of prime minister.

Special Words

Acadia
The area in British North America settled by the French. It is now New Brunswick, Nova Scotia, and Prince Edward Island.

Algonquian
A language spoken by the Northern forest Indians. Algonquian was spoken south and east of the Churchill River.

Athapaskan
A language spoken by the Northern forest Indians. Athapaskan speakers lived northwest of the Churchill River.

bateaux
Large, open boats used to transport goods between Montreal and Lake Ontario.

canots du maitre
Twelve-metre-long canoes made from the bark of the yellow birch with a cedar frame. Although less than 300 pounds in weight when dry, they could carry close to four tons.

canots du nord
Small-goods-carrying canoes used on rivers and smaller lakes. They held about a ton and a half.

coureurs de bois
Canoe-paddling traders who exchanged European goods for the valuable beaver pelts of North America.

emigrate
To leave your own country and settle in another.

Huron
Northern farming Indians of what is now Simcoe County in Ontario. They spoke the Iroquoian language. Five tribes formed the Huron Confederacy.

immigrate
To come into a foreign country as a settler.

Inuit
Native Americans of northern Canada. They hunted the polar bear, seal, whale, and walrus, as well as caribou, bear and musk ox. The Inuit lived in small family groups clustered together.

Iroquois	Northern farming Indians. They spoke an Iroquoian dialect. The Iroquois Confederacy is made up of the Seneca, Cayuga, Oneida, Onondaga, and Mohawk.
Jesuits	The Society of Jesus. A religious group begun in Paris, France, by Ignatius Loyola and others.
métis	Western Canadians of mixed blood. They were the descendants of French and British fur traders and native peoples.
New England	The northeastern members of the Thirteen Colonies on the southeastern border of British North America. They would eventually become part of the United States.
pemmican	A mixture of buffalo fat, meat, and currants pounded and dried. It was first used by the Indians when they were travelling and then by the white explorers and fur traders.
saga	A long story told by northern European peoples such as the Vikings and Celts. It was often about a great hero or voyage.
scurvy	A disease caused by a lack of vitamin C in the diet. Early sailors and settlers often suffered from scurvy.
seigneurial system	A system of granting land in New France. Land was given to a seigneur by the king. The seigneur, in turn, rented it out to settlers who farmed it.
seigneury	A rectangular piece of land granted to a seigneur by the king of France.
Tory	A supporter of the Conservative Party. Tories were traditionally linked to the Church of England.
voyageurs	Paid canoe men who worked for the Eastern merchants in the fur trade.
wampum	A string of shell beads used as money or ornament by some Indian nations.

Index

This index is an alphabetical list of the important words and topics in this book.

When you are looking for a special piece of information, you can look for the word in this list and it will tell you which pages to look at.

Acknowledgement

The publishers of **Childcraft** gratefully acknowledge the following artists, photographers, publishers, agencies and corporations for illustrations used in this volume. All illustrations are the exclusive property of the publishers of **Childcraft** unless names are marked with an asterisk*.

Cover	Barry Wilkinson, B. L. Kearley Limited
2/3	Sarah Figlio
6/7	Trevor Ridley, B. L. Kearley Limited
8/9	Roy King, Specs Art Agency
10/11	Donald Harley, B. L. Kearley Limited
12/13	Charles Front
14/15	Mark Peppé, B. L. Kearley Limited
16/17	Terry Thomas, Specs Art Agency
18/19	Barry Wilkinson, B. L. Kearley Limited
20/21	Roger Wade Walker, Specs Art Agency
22/23	Nick Day
24/25	Roy King, Specs Art Agency
26/27	Roger Wade Walker, Specs Art Agency
28/29	Donald Harley, B. L. Kearley Limited
30/31	Terry Thomas, Specs Art Agency
32/33	Mark Peppé, B. L. Kearley Limited
34/35	Gerald Witcomb, Specs Art Agency
36/37	Shirley Tourret, B. L. Kearley Limited
38/39	Roger Wade Walker, Specs Art Agency
40/41	Roy King, Specs Art Agency
42/43	Charles Front
44/45	Mark Peppé, B. L. Kearley Limited
46/47	Terry Thomas, Specs Art Agency
48/49	Specs Art Agency
50/51	Donald Harley, B. L. Kearley Limited
52/53	Graham Sumner
54/55	Terry Thomas, Specs Art Agency
56/57	Mark Peppé, B. L. Kearley Limited; Linda Kinnaman
58/59	Roy King, Specs Art Agency
60/61	Nigel Alexander
62/63	Barry Wilkinson, B. L. Kearley Limited
64/65	Mark Peppé, B. L. Kearley Limited
66/67	Michael Strand, B. L. Kearley Limited
68/69	Nick Day
70/71	Donald Harley, B. L. Kearley Limited
72/73	Terry Thomas, Specs Art Agency
74/75	Roger Wade Walker, Specs Art Agency
76/77	Barry Wilkinson, B. L. Kearley Limited
78/79	Donald Harley, B. L. Kearley Limited
80/81	Donald Harley, B. L. Kearley Limited
82/83	Roy King, Specs Art Agency
84/85	Donald Harley, B. L. Kearley Limited
86/87	Graham Sumner
88/89	Mark Peppé, B. L. Kearley Limited
90/91	Trevor Ridley, B. L. Kearley Limited
92/93	Robert Geary, B. L. Kearley Limited
94/95	Terry Thomas, Specs Art Agency
96/97	Trevor Ridley, B. L. Kearley Limited
98/99	Trevor Ridley, B. L. Kearley Limited
100/101	Donald Harley, B. L. Kearley Limited
102/103	Roy King, Specs Art Agency
104/105	Barry Wilkinson, B. L. Kearley Limited
106/107	Terry Thomas, Specs Art Agency
108/109	Roger Wade Walker, Specs Art Agency
110/111	Trevor Ridley, B. L. Kearley Limited
112/113	Mark Peppé, B. L. Kearley Limited
114/115	Shirley Bellwood, B. L. Kearley Limited
116/117	Trevor Ridley, B. L. Kearley Limited
118/119	Michael Strand, B. L. Kearley Limited
120/121	Donald Harley, B. L. Kearley Limited
122/123	Mark Peppé, B. L. Kearley Limited
124/125	Joanna Williams, B. L. Kearley Limited
126/127	Terry Thomas, Specs Art Agency
128/129	Richard Berridge
130/131	Charles Front
132/133	Charles Front
134/135	Mark Peppé, B. L. Kearley Limited; Oil painting on canvas (1936), National Gallery of Canada, Ottawa*; Oil painting on wood (1916), Art Gallery of Ontario, gift of Dr. Lorne Pierce, 1958, in memory of Edith Chown Pierce*
136/137	Mark Peppé, B. L. Kearley Limited
138/139	Richard Berridge
140/141	Richard Berridge
142/143	Terry Thomas, Specs Art Agency
144/145	Trevor Ridley, B. L. Kearley Limited
146/147	Roy King, Specs Art Agency
148/149	Zoom/Vandystadt from Allsport*; Ruetters/Bettman*; Canapress*
150/151	Barry Wilkinson, B. L. Kearley Limited
152/153	Canapress*